D1765543

FUNGI

FACING PAGE
Russulaceae
Lactarius aurantiofulvus (x 5)

EVERGREEN is an imprint of Benedikt Taschen Verlag GmbH

© for this edition: 1999 Benedikt Taschen Verlag GmbH
Hohenzollernring 53, D–50672 Köln
© 1998 Editions du Chêne – Hachette Livre – Champignons
Under the direction of Paul Starosta
Text: Christian Epinat
Photographs: Paul Starosta
Text editor: Cécile Aoustin
Layout: Christopher Evans
Translation: Josephine Bacon in association with First Edition Translations Ltd, Cambridge
Realization of the English edition by First Edition Translations Ltd, Cambridge

Printed in Italy
ISBN 3–8228–6515–X

FUNGI

Photographs PAUL STAROSTA
Text CHRISTIAN EPINAT

E
EVERGREEN

Contents

The World of Fungi

Coriolaceae
Trametes versicolor (x 1.3)

Important Note

The notes to the captions have the following meanings:

• *not worth picking*: this mushroom should not be picked for eating purposes, for any of the following reasons:

– because it is inedible (unpleasant taste, tough, etc.)

– because some people cannot digest it

– because it is not known whether or not it is edible

– because the species is too rare

• *edible but risky*: this mushroom can be eaten but only on condition that the picking or preparation advice is strictly complied with.

The asterisk (*) refers to entries in the glossary (p.128).

ungi are the mysterious denizens of our fields and woods. Each autumn, young and old hunt down these capricious growths whose main attraction, for some at least, is that they are edible. A few inquisitive souls attempt to uncover the secret of their lives and are thus led into an amazing world of shapes, colours and smells, a world so vast that no single individual could explore all its treasures in a single lifetime.

Although their cellular structure is akin to that of plants, fungi are classified in a separate kingdom or phylum characterised by nutrition through absorption, as distinct from the plant kingdom, in which nutrition is mainly through photosynthesis, and the animal kingdom, governed by a digestive system. Fungi may adopt three different modes of life — saprophytism, parasitism and symbiosis — in order to obtain the nutrients they need for their development.

Saprophytism

Chlorophyll makes it possible for plants to produce the substances they need for growth, which are based on carbon dioxide and water, by means of the energy of light. Fungi contain no chlorophyll and so they are forced to absorb these substances from their environment. If they feed on dead organisms, they are saprophytes. This is what happens in fields (thanks to dead grass), the forest floor (from leaves, pine-needles, pine-cones, etc.), on tree trunks and the branches of dead trees or even on timber (house beams, ships' timbers, pit-props, etc.). Some fungi prefer to grow on other types of organic matter such as excrement, the corpses of insects, sugary substrates such as fruit and bread or the cellulose content of paper and the tissues of plant fibres.

Parasitism

Fungi which live at the expense of a living organism where the parasitised host is adversely affected by the situation are called parasites. This applies to certain fungi such as polypores (the Sulphur Polypore and the Birch Polypore, for instance) which grow on tree trunks or branches and attack the heart of the tree, causing destructive rot. Grapevine mildew, potato blight, wheat rust and apple canker are other examples of these undesirable fungi. Humans and animals may be superficially parasitised on the phanera* or skin. The effect is more serious if the internal tissues are affected by fungal diseases such as candida, aspergillosis, etc. which are even able to cause death.

Symbiosis occurs where the host benefits from the presence of the fungus and its chances of survival are improved. The best example of symbiosis is lichen (an association between an alga and a fungus). This also applies to myrmecophilous fungi which become food for ants by developing on leaves brought into the ant-hill, or *Termitomyces,* species which colonise termite mounds, an environment which they find favourable, and break down the cellulose and lignin into substances from which the insects can draw nourishment. The mycorrhiza is a network of plant roots and fungus mycelium which enables each to benefit from the absorption capabilities of the other. Examples of this are the Hollow-Footed Bolete (*Boletinus cavipes*), which forms a mycorrhizal association with larch, and the Black Truffle (*Tuber melanosporum*) with the oak. Orchid seeds cannot germinate unless invaded by fungi. Some of these plants, which have lost their chlorophyll, retain the fungus throughout their lifetime (such as the Neottia or Bird's Nest orchid).

HUMANS AND FUNGI:
A BITTER-SWEET RELATIONSHIP

Traces of the Tinderbox Polypore (*Fomes fomentarius*) have been found alongside flint in prehistoric tombs and certainly helped humans make fire. This shows that man soon learned how to make use of fungi. Some surprising

BELOW
Russulaceae
Russula fageticola (x 0.7)

uses have been found for fungi over the years. The Tinderbox Polypore has been used to cauterise and staunch bleeding. The Birch Polypore (*Piptoporus betulinus*) has been used as a razor-strop and the Maze-Gill (*Daedalea quercina*) as a hairbrush; fungi have been used for dyeing fabric and the native North Americans have used them for bodypaint; they have also been used in the form of belts, head-dresses and various types of armour; and as substitutes for tobacco or chewing-gum; they have even been used as perfumes and soaps.

Fungi in all their forms are still in widespread use, first and foremost as a food (chanterelles, truffles, etc.). They are also used in industry as a fermentation agent in the manufacture of yoghurt, wine, beer and cider. They are also used to leaven bread and ripen cheese. The making of sauerkraut involves fermenting cabbage in brine, through the action of a bacterium assisted by two species of *Saccharomyces*. In medicine, antibiotics and alkaloids are extracted from fungi. These include the sclerotium of ergot of rye, which is used to alleviate migraine and uterine bleeding. Fungi are also used to synthesise certain molecules which are too complex to create using standard chemistry techniques. Some species, such as Fly Agaric (*Amanita muscaria*) or the Sickener (*Russula emetica*) are used as homeopathic medicines. The African and Chinese pharmacopoeia also contain medicine derived from fungi. In agriculture, fungi are being developed for use as insecticides and cattle fodder (yeast foodstuffs).

On the other side of the coin, fungi can be man's worst enemy. Most people are aware of the danger of eating the Death Cap (*Amanita phalloides*), which was often used by poisoners (it was one of the substances used by Agrippina to kill the Emperor Claudius). Moulds found on peanuts secrete a carcinogenic substance known as aflatoxin. Ergot of rye (*Claviceps purpurea*) is responsible for the disease known as St Anthony's Fire, whose symptoms are a burning sensation in the extremities, followed by gangrene and atrophy of the limbs, and ending in death. Some fungi are hallucinogenic and are used in certain religious rites and ceremonies, such as those of the Mayas, who sculpted 'stone mushrooms' and ate Psilocybe fungi. Fly Agaric is still used for ritual purposes by native peoples of Siberia. Liberty Caps (*Psilocybe semilanceata*) which grows throughout Europe has hallucinogenic properties. Fungi can also destroy crops, such as the vine (mildew, oidium wilt), fruit trees (rust and smut), vegetables, flowers and even animals. Nor are cooked foods safe, since they have to be preserved against the ravages of fungi by chilling, drying, canning, chemical treatment or even radiation. Wood and its by-products also suffer from fungal destruction (every navy has had its ships put out of action by Dry Rot). For this reason, excessive humidity should be eliminated from houses in order to protect the woodwork, books and fabrics. Libraries, film libraries and museums have to be particularly careful to preserve their

Amanitaceae
Amanita submembranacea (x 1.2)

collections against elements which could cause fragile items to deteriorate, and they do so by means of hygrometry and controlling the light and temperature.

MUSHROOMS ARE FRUITS

Of the 75,000 or so species currently known, those which are particularly fascinating are the so-called higher fungi that grow in the woods and fields and whose mysterious and capricious appearance sometimes mystifies the greatest experts. To get to know these organisms better, their life cycle needs to be studied.

The life of a fungus begins with a microscopic cell called a spore. The only way spores can be seen with the naked eye is to slice off the stem of a mushroom just below the cap and place the cap, gills downwards, on a piece of cartridge paper. After a few hours, a powder will have been deposited which consists of tens of millions of spores (it has been calculated that the Cultivated Mushroom releases 40 million spores an hour). If the same experiment is applied to different types of fungi, it will be noted that the colour of the powder changes depending on the genus — black for Coprinus, white for Amanitas, pink for Entolomas. This feature can help to identify a fungus species. When all of the conditions are right (temperature, humidity, sun, soil type, etc.), the spore germinates and produces a little filament which divides and ramifies to create a network called the mycelium. The mycelium can be seen in the wild in leaf-mould, in the humus of pine forests where it binds the needles together and in the rotten wood which it colonises. Sometimes the mycelium looks like woody strings; these are called rhizomorphs (such as those produced by *Megacollybia platyphylla*). It can also resemble coloured compact masses which may be quite large. These are sclerotia which function as storage bodies. In most cases, the mycelium consists of thin, invisible threads which remain hidden in the soil. It may last for several days if the substrate on which it feeds is soon broken down and is not renewable, as in the case of Coprinus species living on farmyard waste. Fungi which grow in the soil, and thus have a limitless substrate, survive for many years (even for centuries, according to some writers!). They remain associated with the tree-roots with which they have formed a mycorrhiza or extend outwards in search of

ABOVE
Hygrophoraceae
Hygrocybe mucronella (× 2)

food. When all the factors are present which are propitious for reproduction, the mycelium created from a spore fuses with the mycelium of another spore and which is of a compatible 'sex'. The result of this fusion is a secondary, fertile mycelium, which produces a fungus. The correct name for this part of the fungus is the fruiting body. It is a type of fruit, which emerges from the substrate and is created from a mass of the filaments of the mycelium which are used for the specialist task of producing cells that specialise in making spores. The cycle is complete. In some species, such as the Fairy Ring Champignon (*Marasmius oreades*), St George's Mushroom (*Calocybe gambosa*), the bolete known as *Suillus granulatus*, the Clouded Agaric (*Clitocybe nebularis*) and the Clitocybe known as *Lepista inversa*, as the nutrients are drawn from the soil, the mycelium radiates in a circle from a central point which is the fertile mycelium. The result, which can be seen after a few years, is a ring of fungi, a strange configuration given the name 'fairy ring'. The actual fruiting is of very variable duration, but is always long enough to enable the spores to be dispersed efficiently into the surrounding environment. The time between the appearance of the fruiting body and its rotting away may be a few hours in the case of certain fimicolous* species of Coprinus, two or three months for Morels, and a few years for certain long-lived polypores such as the Tinderbox Fungus. The formation of the fruiting body requires a lot of energy, as can be seen from the Pavement Agaric (*Agaricus bitorquis*), which can often be seen in towns and is easily crushed underfoot and yet is capable of pushing through the asphalt in order to find daylight.

An infinity of shapes and sizes has thus been exploited by nature in order to enable the fungus to succeed at this critical stage. They range from the tiny cup of *Hymenoscyphus fructigenus*, only a few millimetres in diameter, which grows in clusters of several dozen specimens on a single acorn cup, right up to the Giant Puffball (*Langermannia gigantea*), a round mass which can reach 50 cm (20 in) in diameter and is easy to spot in fields. Opinions differ as to the conditions which trigger this phase of reproduction. Some experts believe that the mycelium transforms itself when it is in the peak of condition and has stored sufficient reserves. According to the opposite theory, fruiting occurs only when the mycelium meets conditions which make it harder and harder for it to survive. It then seeks to perpetuate itself by producing spores, a very hardy life form capable of surviving unfavourable climatic conditions for a long time. It has been shown that the spores of some species retain their ability to germinate for several decades.

THE UBIQUITY OF FUNGI

It is difficult to determine the habitat of all the living things which are included in the phylum of fungi. Some, such as *Aspergillus* or *Penicillium* moulds, are found in the soil, even at great depths in the case of species which can tolerate an absence of light or oxygen. They may parasitise algae, fish and shellfish in fresh or salt water. Fungus spores are found in the atmosphere, even at high altitudes. Some prefer the cold, living in polar ice, others prefer heat and live in compost. The habitat of the macrofungi, the so-called higher fungi, is more restricted. Most of them grow in warm, humid places. Their numbers rapidly diminish in the extreme temperatures of very high mountains, the poles or the deserts (in which there is also a lack of water). Wind is also a great enemy of fungi.

Some species are found almost throughout the world, such as the Cep or Penny Bun Mushroom (*Boletus edulis*) which grows in places as far apart as France, Egypt, Canada and Japan, but the plethora of ecological conditions on our planet also creates very specific flora. There are thus species specific to the arctic tundras, the deserts, high mountains and equatorial forests.

CHEMICAL COMPOSITION

A fleshy fungus contains an average of 75 to 85% water. The ratio is lower in woody species and a great deal higher (more than 90%) in gelatinous species. The remaining dry matter can be divided into proteins (2 to 5%), carbohydrates (2 to 13%), lipids (1 to 2%), trace elements (0.5 to 2%, potassium, calcium, phosphorus, magnesium, silica, iron, copper, etc.) and vitamins (A, B_1, B_2, C, D, etc.). Enzymes, fragrances and sapids, colouring agents, etc. may also be present as well as resins and numerous other substances which can produce extraordinary natural phenomena such as luminescence (the gills of a fresh Olive-Tree Pleurotus are luminous in the dark).

The chemical composition can also be used to determine the species. In order to identify a fungus, a mycologist carefully observes the distribution of the various pigments in all its parts, also taking account of any colour change resulting from the action of natural factors. For instance, the Black Russula (*Russula nigricans*) has white flesh which first reddens then darkens on exposure to air; the Red-Footed Boletus (*Boletus erythropus*) has

OPPOSITE
Fistulinaceae
Fistulina hepatica (× 2)

ABOVE
Coriolaceae
Oligoporus caesius (x 0.75)

yellow flesh which turns blue when exposed to air; *Lactarius chrysorrheus* has white milk which turns golden in the air; the gills of the Spotted Gomphidius (*Gomphidius maculatus*) redden when rubbed. Fungi may change colour through having chemicals applied to them, such as alkalis, acids, iodine, iron sulphate or aniline. The yellow flesh of certain species of Cortinarius reddens when sodium is applied to it, the flesh of certain Russulas turns green or pink under the action of iron sulphate, and the spores of Amanita species blacken in contact with iodine. It may also often be necessary to taste a fragment of the flesh to help in identification, to see whether a red Russula is acrid or mild, or whether the milk of a brown species of Lactarius is mild or peppery. A strong odour is also very helpful and may identify the species immediately. *Clitocybe odora* smells of aniseed and *Mycena pura* smells of radishes; *Inocybe cervicolor* also smells of radishes and *Mycena stipata* smells of bleach. Certain species of *Marasmius* smell of garlic or cabbage, and so on.

FUNGI SHOULD BE TREATED WITH CARE

A large number of fungi are poisonous, and some of the substances of which they consist are harmful to man. Any species intended for eating must be carefully identified if a range of unpleasant side-effects, from slight stomach upsets to serious and even fatal illness, is to be avoided. The amount of time that elapses before the symptoms appear is an indication of their seriousness. If there are signs in less than six hours, the

matter is unlikely to be serious. If symptoms appear only after this amount of time, there is a danger of serious poisoning. Poisonous fungi can be classified in six groups, based on the symptoms they produce.

Gastro-intestinal upsets

Where these are the only symptom, they may be due to an individual intolerance which certain fungi, such as the Yellow-staining Mushroom (*Agaricus xanthodermus*) and the Mist Fungus (*Clitocybe nebularis*), are inclined to produce. On the other hand there are some genuinely poisonous species, including the Devil's Bolete (*Boletus satanas*), the Olive-tree Pleurotus (*Omphalotus olearius*), the Tiger-stripe Tricholoma (*Tricholoma pardinum*) and the Livid Entoloma (*Entoloma sinuatum*), that have been responsible for violent and painful stomach upsets (vomiting, diarrhœa, etc.) that appear less than six hours after eating. The Beautiful Coral Fungus (*Ramaria formosa*) has a highly purgative action.

Gastro-intestinal upsets accompanied by nervous symptoms

Fly Agaric (*Amanita muscaria*) and the Panther Cap (*Amanita pantherina*) cause stomach upsets followed by agitation, an excited state and sometimes delirium; some species of Psilocybe, Stropharia, Paneola and Conocybe have hallucinogenic properties. Some small white species of Clitocybe and Inocybe produce hypersecretions of perspiration, saliva and tears. These symptoms also appear rapidly (in less than six hours).

Vascular symptoms

This group contains several species of Coprinus, especially the Common Ink Cap (*Coprinus atramentarius*) and the Club-foot (*Clitocybe clavipes*). These fungi will produce reddening and hot flushes due to vasodilation in just a few minutes if they are consumed with alcohol.

Hæmolysis (destruction of the red blood cells)

This problem is caused mainly by Morels, Helvellas, and certain species of Amanita such as The Blusher (*Amanita rubescens*) if they are eaten raw or undercooked. Thorough cooking, especially boiling, will eliminate any risk. The boiling water should be discarded.

Serious poisonings with delayed symptoms

The False Morel (*Gyromitra esculenta*) should always be blanched and the cooking water discarded. If it is undercooked or left in its cooking juices, it can produce unpleasant gastro-intestinal symptoms after a minimum of eight hours. There may be fever, delirium and even liver damage. Some Helvella species can produce the same symptoms. The Death Cap (*Amanita phalloides*), the Spring Amanita (*Amanita verna*), the Destroying Angel (*Amanita virosa*), and a few small species of Lepiota such as *Lepiota helveola* or *Lepiota brunneoincarnata,* as well as the Marginal Pholiota (*Galerina marginata*) and similar species can kill in three days by causing liver damage. The Annatto-coloured Cortinarius (*Cortinarius orellanus*) and *Cortinarius speciosissimus* have been responsible for kidney failure.

Poisoning by the Brown Roll-rim (*Paxillus involutus*)

This very common species must be eaten several times before it causes serious indigestion which manifests itself rapidly. Both the liver and kidneys are affected. The poisoning appears to be the result of an immunological reaction caused by sensitivity to certain toxic elements in the fungus. The consequences can be fatal.

The only way to avoid poisoning is to be absolutely sure which species are edible. It is no use relying on the old adage that fungi which are eaten by insects and slugs are not poisonous, because these creatures are able to consume the deadliest fungi without apparent harm. The most dangerous fallacy is that a silver coin or spoon will blacken when cooked with a poisonous mushroom. Furthermore, fungi that are toxic remain so, even if boiled, salted or pickled in vinegar.

Pollution may also be the reason for certain cases of poisoning. Fungi have the ability to store pollutants, such as heavy metals, defoliants and radioactive substances, in their tissues. It is therefore wise to avoid picking those which grow in places where there is a risk of pollution, such as in cities, industrial areas, and in and around cultivated fields.

A VERY PERISHABLE FOODSTUFF

The heavy concentration of water in a mushroom explains why it does not have good keeping qualities. A minimum number of precautions need to be taken when picking and preparing fungi for the table.

– Only the youngest and freshest specimens should be picked, especially in the case of species which grow in clumps, those which are more resistant to frost or any that dry out and swell up again after heavy rain.

– Never carry fungi in plastic or polythene bags as this accelerates their putrefaction; use an open basket.

– Cook or preserve fungi as quickly as possible (do not keep them in the refrigerator for more than 24 hours).

Various techniques can be used depending on the texture of the fungus. They may be deep-frozen, dried, cooked, pickled in a strong vinegar solution and potted, or they may be salted or canned in preserving jars.

A mushroom which is too old, poorly preserved or undercooked will behave in the same way as rotten meat and can produce serious gastro-intestinal symptoms which may even lead to death. Fungi are not easy to digest, especially if combined with fat, so fried and fricasseed mushrooms should be consumed in small amounts. Even though a few fungi can be consumed raw, such as the Amanita of the Caesars (*Amanita caesarea*) or the Jelly Tongue (*Pseudohydnum gelatinosum*), or used as seasonings (Black and White Truffles, the Fairy Ring Mushroom, the Garlic-scented Marasmius), most should be thoroughly cooked before eating. The extremely perishable nature of this foodstuff also means that in many countries the sale of fungi is strictly controlled. Cultivated mushrooms are subject to the same legislation as fruit and vegetables. Local authorities in some countries decide which species may be sold and they may appoint an inspector to ensure that the regulations are observed. However, if you are sure of the species you have collected, here are a few simple and delicious recipes:

FACING PAGE
Entolomataceae
Entoloma nitidum (x 5)

RIGHT
Boletaceae
Suillus grevillei (x 2.2)

Raw Mushroom Salad

Only certain species can be eaten raw, including the Amanita of the Caesars, the Beefsteak Fungus (*Fistulina hepatica*), the Jelly Fungus (*Tremelodon gelatinosum*) and the cultivated mushroom (*Agaricus bisporus*).
Slice them thinly into strips and sprinkle with oil flavoured with lemon and parsley.

Champignons à la Grecque

Button mushrooms are simmered in a mixture of oil and white wine, to which lemon juice and tomato purée are added.

Chanterelles in Butter

Cook the Chanterelles in butter, adding a chopped shallot, garlic and parsley.

Fairy Ring Omelette

Sauté Fairy Ring Champignon caps in butter and add them to the beaten eggs before cooking.

Morels in Cream Sauce

Braise the Morels in butter with onions, then simmer in a Béchamel sauce thickened with crème fraîche.

Truffes en Papillotes

Marinate the truffles in cognac, then wrap them in lean bacon rashers and wrap loosely in a paper bag before cooking in the oven.

BELOW
Cantharellaceae
Cantharellus cibarius (x 1)

NOMENCLATURE: THE BINOMIAL SYSTEM

By observing characteristics which are increasingly precise and selective, a classification is obtained which, like a pyramid, culminates in a final indivisible stage – the species. A species is defined as a group of individuals which are morphologically identical and which can breed with each other. The main stages of this pyramid, in decreasing order of size, are: the division, the class, the order, the family, the genus (pl. genera) and the species. For instance, in the case of the Chestnut Bolete (*Gyroporus castaneus*), this produces:
Division: Basidiomycota; class: Basidiomycetes; order: Boletales; family: Gyrodontaceae; genus: Gyroporus; species: *castaneus.*
This very specific name follows the rules of the International Code of Botanical Nomenclature.
In practice, each fungus is designated by the name of the genus, followed by the name of the species, both of which are in Latin. These are followed by the name or names of the mycologist or mycologists who helped to create the name of the species in question. The Chestnut Bolete was first described and named *Boletus castaneus* by Bulliard (Bull.) in 1791. This description became outdated and could have led to confusion, but the *Boletus castaneus* named by Fries (Fr.), a more recent mushroom expert (1821), was retained for this fungus; in 1886, Quélet proposed the genus *Gyroporus* in which he placed the Chestnut Bolete. The result is thus *Gyroporus castaneus* (Bull.: Fr.) Quel. The names are carefully chosen by taxonomists as a reminder of the significant characteristics of a species. Thus *Gyroporus* refers to the rounded shape of the pores and *castaneus* to the chestnut colour of the cap of this fungus. Sometimes the latinised name of a famous mycologist is adopted for a species, as in the case of *Boletus queletii* (Quélet's Bolete).

MYCOLOGY, A RECENT SCIENCE

The art of fungus identification and toxicology is directly linked to scientific advances. In antiquity, the only fungi eaten were the Amanita of the Caesars, the Cep and the Truffle. Accidental poisonings which were the cause of death of several notable figures in Greece and Rome,

ABOVE
Tricholomataceae
Flammulina velutipes (x 1.3)

such as Euripides whose family was decimated by eating poisonous Amanitas, show that knowledge of the subject was limited. The Death Cap was already known to be fatal, however, and was used as a poison. Progress in the Middle Ages was negligible. Mushroom poisonings continued (as in the case of Pope Clement VII in 1534). The first efforts at description and compilation of knowledge began in the sixteenth century. The treatise produced by the French botanist Charles de l'Écluse, mentioning about a hundred species, is evidence of this. Progress continued in the eighteenth century with Micheli, Paulet and Battara among others. The nineteenth century saw a sudden burst of interest. Perhaps the most outstanding of this generation of mycologists is the Swede Elias Fries, whose work served as the basis for modern scientific nomenclature. The microscope soon became indispensable for identification purposes and made it possible to produce even more accurate descriptions. The founding of mycological societies encouraged contact between mycologists. In the twentieth century, improved transport facilities made it possible to increase exchanges of knowledge and made it easier to engage in field studies. Photography added a visual aid to the descriptions. As computerisation develops to new heights in the twenty-first century, an ever larger pool of knowledge will be available to more and more people. Information will be well organised and more compact and available throughout the world. As the science of genetics progresses, taxonomy and classification will become even more precise and knowledge of the various species will increase, as new characteristics are added to their description.

Fig.1

Boletales

There are about 500 species of bolete worldwide. Their distinguishing feature is a cap, the underside of which is covered with a mass of parallel tubes which have pore-like downward-facing openings. The tubes are easily separable from the flesh of the fungus. All the European boletes grow on the ground, with the exception of *Pulveroboletus lignicola* which grows on conifers and the Parasitical Bolete (*Xerocomus parasiticus*) which grows on the fungi called Earthballs (*Scleroderma*). The best-known and tastiest bolete is the Cep or Penny Bun Mushroom. The best way to identify the various species is through the host tree (many of the species being mycorrhizal), the colour of the pores (white, yellow, red, etc.), the colour and texture of the cap (whether it is slimy or velvety, etc.) and the colour and decoration of the stem (whether it has a network of veins, a ring, etc.). The flesh of many boletes turns blue when broken. This is an enzymatic reaction which changes certain invisible constituents (gyrocyanine, variegatic acid, xerocomic acid, etc.) into blue derivatives. It has nothing to do with edibility, because the Devil's Bolete (*Boletus satanas*) turns slightly blue and is not edible, while *Boletus erythropus* produces a bright blue colour and is delicious when thoroughly cooked.

FACING PAGE

Boletaceae

Suillus grevillei (x 3.5)

The Larch Bolete has a cap about 10 cm (4 in) in diameter, which varies in colour from golden to orange-brown. It is smooth, shiny and viscous. The pores are straight and yellow, showing patches of reddish-grey when touched. The stem is yellow above the whitish cottony ring, the top of which has a network of lines. The yellowish flesh gradually marbles pinky-violet with age.

GROWING SEASON: summer – autumn

HABITAT: under larches

FREQUENCY: very common in its habitat

EDIBILITY: of little value

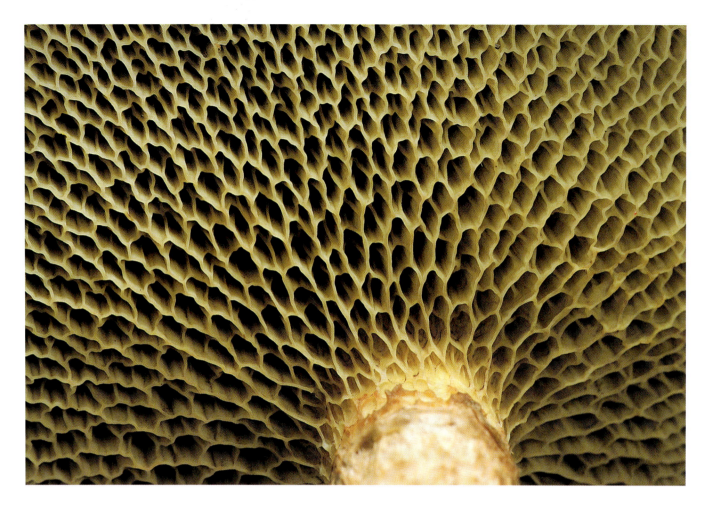

Gyrodontaceae

Boletinus cavipes (x 3.6)

The Hollow-stemmed Bolete has a striking 10 cm (4 in) wide reddish-brown cap entirely covered with little fibrous scales. The olive-coloured pores are initially covered by a white veil in the young specimen and extend down the stem. The stem is yellow-brown, fibrilose below the ring and becomes hollow at an early stage, hence the common name of the fungus. There is a subspecies which is entirely bright yellow in colour.

GROWING SEASON: summer – autumn

HABITAT: under larches

FREQUENCY: infrequent

EDIBILITY: not worth picking

Boletaceae

Boletus pinophilus (x 1.8)

The Pine Bolete is very similar to the Cep or Penny Bun (*Boletus edulis*). The fleshy cap is dark reddish-brown, and may be smooth or velvety. The stem is swollen and is covered in a whitish network of lines on a reddish background. The pores are white then turn greenish-yellow. The white flesh does not turn blue when exposed to air. Not to be confused with the Bitter Bolete (*Tylopilus felleus*), whose pores are pinkish, but which is inedible due to its bitterness.

GROWING SEASON: summer – autumn

HABITAT: conifers (especially pines), mixed forests

FREQUENCY: fairly common

EDIBILITY: excellent

Strobilomycetaceae

Strobilomyces strobilaceus (x 2)

No doubt the most unusual-looking bolete, so much so that it is immediately identifiable, the Pine-cone Bolete owes its name to the cap which is covered in large greyish-brown woolly scales. The stem is the same colour and is woolly and furry. The grey, angular pores sometimes turn reddish-brown when touched. The whitish flesh turns pink at first then darkens to slate grey on old specimens.

GROWING SEASON: summer – autumn

HABITAT: beech woods and conifers

FREQUENCY: fairly rare

EDIBILITY: not worth picking

Fungi

ABOVE

Boletaceae

Boletus satanas (x 1)

The Devil's Bolete has a dirty white cap on a thickened stem which is yellowish at the top and reddish at the base, covered in a network of fine red lines. The pores are yellow at first, then red. The flesh is yellowish, turning blue, and the fungus is said to have a rubbery smell.

GROWING SEASON: summer – autumn

HABITAT: warm leaf-mould on
chalky soil

FREQUENCY: rare

EDIBILITY: poisonous

FACING

Boletaceae

Suillus bovinus (x 1)

This bolete has a sticky, slimy, brownish-yellow to brownish-orange cap about 10 cm (4 in) in diameter. The pores are quite large and are dirty yellow in colour. The sinuous stem sometimes ends in pink mycelium. The flesh is yellowish, soft and elastic. It tends to grow in clumps.

GROWING SEASON: summer – autumn

HABITAT: pine woods

FREQUENCY: common

EDIBILITY: not recommended

Fungi

Agaricales

Agaricales are soft-fleshed fungi with caps whose undersides are covered with sets of gills which radiate from stems that are normally central. They may take the classic shape of an open umbrella, as in the case of the Fly Agaric (*Amanita muscaria*) or they may be funnel-shaped as in the case of the Fleecy Milk-cap (*Lactarius vellereus*). The stem may be lateral or may even disappear altogether as in the Pleurotas. Agaricales are divided into various genera, mainly on the basis of the colour and shape of their spores, the manner in which the gills are attached to the stem and the type of veil which may be present (ring, cortina, etc.) and the presence of cells of characteristic type, especially in the cuticle of the cap and on the gills. The group contains about 8,000 species; it includes most of the cultivated varieties as well as the largest number of poisonous species, such as the Death Cap (*Amanita phalloides*). The oldest known example of an Agaric was found preserved in resin and is about 90 million years old. It looks like a little Fairy Ring Champignon with a cap about 3.2 mm (⅛ in) in diameter!

FACING PAGE

Pleurotaceae

Pleurotus ostreatus (x 2.1)

The Oyster Mushroom attaches itself to wood on a short lateral stem. The shell-shaped cap may attain 20 cm (8 in) in diameter and is smooth and fleshy. It varies in colour between beige and brownish-violet or blue-grey. The gills are whitish as is the flesh. The Oyster Mushroom normally grows in clumps. It is easy to cultivate, and is now grown commercially.

GROWING SEASON: autumn – winter

HABITAT: on wood

FREQUENCY: fairly common

EDIBILITY: excellent

Fig. 2

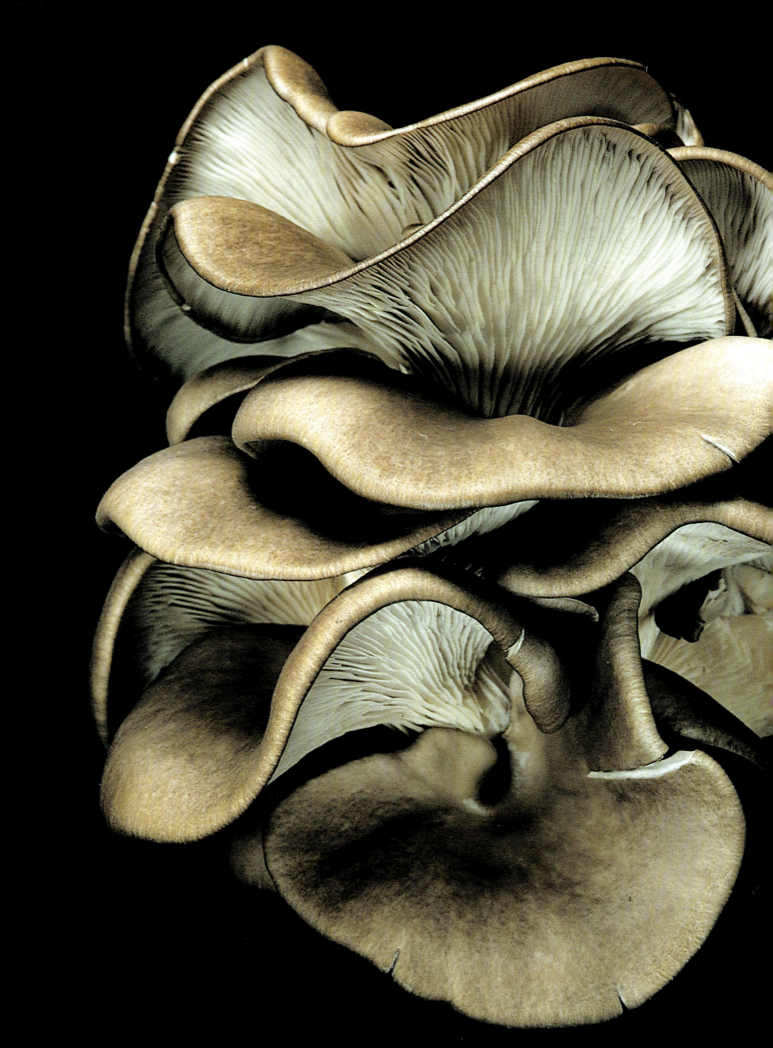

Paxillaceae

Paxillus filamentosus (x 0.9)

The cap is 10 – 15 cm (4 – 6 in) in diameter and may be flat or slightly depressed in the centre. It is yellowish-brown, with radial striations at the margin. The ochraceous yellow gills are decurrent. They separate easily from the flesh and turn brown when rubbed, as do the yellow stem and the flesh. This fungus, like its close relation the Roll Rim (*Paxillus involutus*), is poisonous.

GROWING SEASON: summer – autumn

HABITAT: under alders

FREQUENCY: fairly common in its habitat

EDIBILITY: poisonous

Paxillaceae

Omphalotus olearius (x 1.1)

The Olive-tree Pleurotus is a handsome species with a depressed or funnel-shaped cap which may reach 15 cm (6 in) in diameter. The cap is yellow-orange or brownish-orange and with fine radial fibrillations. The gills are orange in colour but paler than the cap, strongly decurrent and the same colour as the stem, which is often excentric and tapering. This fungus normally grows in clumps at the foot of tree-trunks or stumps. It may also be found growing on the ground in contact with buried roots.

GROWING SEASON: autumn – winter

HABITAT: under olive trees

FREQUENCY: common around the Mediterranean

EDIBILITY: poisonous

Fungi

Gomphidiaceae

Gomphidius glutinosus (x 2.3)

This fungus, known as Cow's Muzzle (*mufle de vache*) in French, has a cap about 10 cm (4 in) in diameter which is greyish-violet in colour and covered with a sticky, shiny veil. The thick gills are strongly decurrent; they are white when young but soon turn grey then black as the spores ripen. The stem is viscous, white at the top and bright yellow at the base. A closely related species, *Gomphidius maculatus*, grows under larches, but has a flecked cap and gills which redden when rubbed.

GROWING SEASON: summer – autumn

HABITAT: conifers (especially spruces)

FREQUENCY: fairly common

EDIBILITY: edible

Russulaceae

Lactarius deterrimus (x 3.5)

This species closely resembles the Saffron Milk-cap (*Lactarius deliciosus*) which only grows under pines, and has the same 'carrot-coloured' milk which it exudes when broken. However, in addition to having a different habitat, this Milk-cap has a smooth stem which is white at the top and more markedly green at the bottom. Other Milk-caps are the Vinous Milk-cap (*Lactarius vinosus*), notable for its lilac-coloured gills and wine-coloured milk, and the Sanguine Milk-cap (*Lactarius sanguifluus*), whose milk is blood-red. All these are edible. However, some may be parasitised on the gills by a white fungus, *Peckiella deformans*.

GROWING SEASON: summer – autumn

HABITAT: spruces

FREQUENCY: fairly common

EDIBILITY: edible

ABOVE

Russulaceae

Lactarius decipiens (x 2.6)

The Deceiver has a cap 3 – 6 cm (1 – 2½ in) in diameter, rosy-beige or brick red in colour, depending on how waterlogged the site is, and a stem of the same colour which darkens towards the base. The gills are pale pinkish-cream. The whitish milk yellows on the gills within a few minutes of picking. If it is placed on a handkerchief, the reaction can be seen in a few seconds. The fungus has the distinctive smell of geranium.

GROWING SEASON: summer – autumn

HABITAT: mainly under hornbeam or oak, occasionally found under conifers

FREQUENCY: fairly common

EDIBILITY: not worth picking

Fungi

Russulaceae

Lactarius torminosus (x 5.25)

The Woolly Milk-Cap is a handsome my-corrhizal species, which is easy to spot when growing. The cap is brick-red with darker concentric circles and may reach a diameter of 15 cm (6 in). The margin remains inrolled until the fungus is fully mature and is covered with woolly fibres.

The stem is white to pink in colour and is often covered in tiny indentations. The flesh is very acrid and exudes a white milk, so it is not suitable for eating. It is easy to distinguish from the Saffron Milk-cap whose milk is orange and which has a cap with a smooth edge.

GROWING SEASON: summer – autumn
HABITAT: under birch trees
FREQUENCY: fairly common
in its habitat
EDIBILITY: poisonous

Fungi

Russulaceae

Russula foetens

The Fœtid Russula may grow to 20 cm (8 in) in diameter. The cap varies from ochre-brown to reddish-beige and the margin is ribbed, viscous and glutinous. The reddish-white stem soon becomes hollow, and the gills are whitish. It has an unpleasant smell of burnt horn.

GROWING SEASON: summer – autumn

HABITAT: all types of wood

FREQUENCY: fairly common

EDIBILITY: not worth picking

Russulaceae

Russula drimeia (x 1)

This Russula has a violet cap which may attain 10 cm (4 in) in diameter. The stem is purplish-lilac in colour. The gills are pale yellow and turn pink in the presence of ammonia. Yellow- or green-capped Russulas exhibiting the same reaction are varieties of this fungus.

GROWING SEASON: summer – autumn

HABITAT: pine woods

FREQUENCY: fairly common

EDIBILITY: not worth picking

Russulaceae

Russula mustelina (x 0.6)

This Russula has an ochraceous-brown cap 10 – 15 cm (4 – 6 in) in diameter on a white stem. The gills are cream-coloured and the flesh is white.

GROWING SEASON: summer – autumn

HABITAT: mountain conifers

FREQUENCY: depends on the region

EDIBILITY: good to eat

Agaricales

Hygrophoraceae

Hygrocybe conicoides (x 5.7)

This Hygrophorus has a conical cap which blackens at the tip. Grains of sand tend to stick to the orange-red, slightly viscous cap. The gills are yellow-orange to salmon-pink, and the straight stem is white or pale yellow, and blackens at the base with age, as does the orange flesh.

GROWING SEASON: autumn

HABITAT: sand-dunes by the sea

FREQUENCY: rare

EDIBILITY: not worth picking

ABOVE

Russulaceae

Russula ochroleuca (x 1.4)

The cap of the Common Yellow Russula may reach 10 cm (4 in) in diameter and is yellow or reddish, in contrast to the white gills and stem. The white flesh is slightly acrid. It is easy to identify due to its distinctive colouring.

GROWING SEASON: summer – autumn

HABITAT: woodland

FREQUENCY: common

EDIBILITY: not worth picking

FACING

Hygrophoraceae

Hygrocybe conica (x 1.6)

The Conical Wax-cap consists of a cap coloured in shades of red to yellow and about 4 cm (2 in) in diameter. It is conical, smooth to fibrillose and slightly viscous in wet weather. The gills are white to yellow in colour. The fragile, striated stem is yellow or orange and whitish at the base. The flesh is whitish at first then coloured under the surface of the cap. The fungus blackens with age or when damaged. It is considered suspect.

GROWING SEASON: summer – autumn

HABITAT: meadows, wet or mossy woods

FREQUENCY: fairly common

EDIBILITY: not worth picking

Fungi

Hygrophoraceae

Hygrophorus marzuolus (x 1.5)

The March Hygrophorus indicates its growing season in its name. It is hard to find because it grows in clumps in wooded areas, usually under a carpet of pine-needles and leaves. The cap is 10 – 15 cm (4 – 6 in) in diameter and is slightly vis-cous in wet weather. It is white at first but darkens with age. The gills are white, darkening to grey. The stem is whitish-grey. The firm flesh is whitish and grey on the surface.

GROWING SEASON: winter – spring

HABITAT: conifers and beech

FREQUENCY: fairly rare

EDIBILITY: good to eat

Hygrophoraceae

Hygrophorus persoonii (x 4.6)

This Hygrophorus has a glutinous cuticle, which is dark olive-brown in colour, and whitish gills. Its cap is 4 – 8 cm (2 – 3 in) in diameter. The fusiform stem is white at the top and covered around the ring with a glutinous veil which produces variega-tions when it tears. It is also characterised by a green reaction to ammonia. The related *H. latitabundus* grows in pine forests on chalky soils and is good to eat.

GROWING SEASON: autumn

HABITAT: broad-leaved trees (oaks, beech)

FREQUENCY: fairly common

EDIBILITY: not worth picking

Tricholomataceae

Panellus serotinus (x 2.5)

The kidney-shaped velvety cap is about
10 cm (4 in) in diameter and is olive-
green in colour, shading to ochraceous
brown in the centre. The gills are of a
contrasting pale yellow-orange. The
stem is short and lateral and is hairy and
scaly. The texture of the flesh becomes
gelatinous in wet weather.

GROWING SEASON: spring – autumn

HABITAT: mainly broad-leaved
trees

FREQUENCY: uncommon

EDIBILITY: not worth picking

Tricholomataceae

Rickenella fibula (x 8)

Despite its small size, a casual stroller can
easily spot this curiosity thanks to its
overall bright orange colour, which contrasts with the surrounding greenery.
The cap is slightly umbilical, and is
barely a centimetre (¼ in) in diameter.
The long, thin stem is a paler extension
of the gills.

GROWING SEASON: spring – autumn

HABITAT: mosses
and grassy places

FREQUENCY: fairly common

EDIBILITY: not worth picking

Fungi

Tricholomataceae

Clitocybe nebularis (x 2.3)

The Clouded Agaric is recognisable by its greyish, fleshy cap which can exceed 20 cm (8 in) in diameter and which is covered in a bloom which later disappears. The pale grey stem is thick and soon softens and the creamy yellow gills are barely decurrent. It has a strong, unpleasant smell. It often forms fairy rings and may cause stomach upsets.

GROWING SEASON: autumn – winter

HABITAT: broad-leaved trees

FREQUENCY: common

EDIBILITY: not worth picking

Tricholomataceae

Lepista nuda (x 1.6)

The Wood Blewit is a species that is sold commercially. The cap is 15 – 20 cm (6 – 8 in) in diameter, and is violet to lilac coloured at first, browning in the centre with age. The closely packed gills are at first deep violet, turning to pale brown in older specimens. They are easily separated from the cap. The fleshy, fibrillose stem is violet at first, but turns pale with age. The Wood Blewit has a strong smell, described as fruity or as smelling like Vitamin B_{12}.

GROWING SEASON: almost year-round, weather permitting

HABITAT: conifers, broad-leaved trees, meadows

FREQUENCY: common

EDIBILITY: good to eat

Agaricales

Tricholomataceae
Tricholoma caligatum (x 2.75)

Although a popular edible fungus in Japan, this Tricholoma is less prized in Europe. It is a large species, the cap being capable of attaining 20 cm (8 in) in diameter. The cap is covered with large reddish-brown fibrillose scales, arranged concentrically on a cream background. The stem has a ring which separates from the white upper part (the gills are also white); the lower part of the stem is identical to the cap. The whole effect is like a sock covering a foot. The fungus exudes a strong, fruity smell which is rather sickly, reminiscent of jasmine or balsam.

GROWING SEASON: summer – autumn
HABITAT: conifers (especially pines), holm-oaks
FREQUENCY: quite rare
EDIBILITY: poor eating quality

ABOVE

Tricholomataceae
Tricholoma myomyces (x 2.5)

The Mouse Grey Tricholoma takes its name from its pale grey cap which may attain 8 cm (3 in) in diameter. The surface is fibrillose to woolly. The gills are whitish-cream. The whitish stem is often covered in a dark cortina.

GROWING SEASON: autumn
HABITAT: pines, woodland
FREQUENCY: fairly common
EDIBILITY: edible

FACING

Tricholomataceae
Tricholoma sulfureum (x 2.9)

The Sulphur Toadstool resembles *Tricholoma equestre* in its sulphurous colouring. It is distinguished by its cap, which may reach 10 cm (4 in) in diameter and is always dry, never viscous, and its more widely spaced gills. The Sulphur Toadstool has a strong smell which has been described as gaseous.

GROWING SEASON: summer – autumn
HABITAT: especially broad-leaved trees
FREQUENCY: common
EDIBILITY: not worth picking

Tricholomataceae

Oudemansiella pudens (x 2.6)

The grey, velvety cap can measure up to 10 cm (4 in) in diameter. The whitish gills are wide and the flesh is white and coriaceous. The velvety stem is very long and slim and is extended by a 'root' which is in contact with buried wood. *Oudemansiella melanotricha*, a very similar species, is found under conifers.

GROWING SEASON: summer – autumn

HABITAT: broad-leaved trees

FREQUENCY: quite rare

EDIBILITY: not worth picking

Tricholomataceae

Oudemansiella mediterranea (x 3.3)

This little fungus has a smooth, sticky cap 1 – 3 cm (¼ – 1 in) in diameter which tends to collect grains of sand. The colour ranges from beige-fawn to reddish-brown. The gills are whitish, thick and widely spaced. The beige stem is elastic, darkening at the base and strongly radicating.

GROWING SEASON: autumn – winter

HABITAT: coastal sands

FREQUENCY: rare

EDIBILITY: not worth picking

Tricholomataceae

Marasmiellus rameatis (x 3)

This Marasmius tends to populate bark and twigs in large colonies. The cap is less than 2 cm (¾ in) in diameter and is white with a brownish or brownish-pink centre. It can be seen to be hairy or velvety under a magnifying glass. The gills are whitish to pink and the stem is pinkish-white at the top darkening to brown towards the base. The magnifying glass reveals the stem to be covered in squamules (tiny scales).

GROWING SEASON: spring – summer – autumn

HABITAT: on twigs

FREQUENCY: fairly common

EDIBILITY: not worth picking

Tricholomataceae

Marasmius quercophilus (x 2.75)

The cap is less than 1 cm (½ in) across, varying from whitish to brownish-pink, depending on the humidity. The gills are whitish and well-shaped. The stem is thin, woolly when young but smoothing with age, whitish at the top, shading to reddish-brown. The fungus has no smell.

GROWING SEASON: summer – autumn

HABITAT: oak leaves and chestnut leaves

FREQUENCY: fairly common in its habitat

EDIBILITY: not worth picking

ABOVE

Tricholomataceae

Megacollybia platyphylla (x 0.5)

This species has a grey-brown cap which attains 20 cm (8 in) in diameter and is decorated with radiating fibrils. The gills are wide and whitish, sometimes streaked with brown. It has a whitish stem which is often extended by as much as several metres (yards) into an extensive subterranean network of whitish mycelial cords known as rhizomorphs.

GROWING SEASON: spring – summer – autumn

HABITAT: Broad-leaved trees, rarely conifers

FREQUENCY: fairly common

EDIBILITY: not worth picking

Tricholomataceae

Mycena epipterygia (x 4.3)

The conical cap is 2 cm (¾ in) in diameter and is whitish, pale yellow or greyish-brown, depending on the variety. It is covered with an elastic, viscous skin which separates easily from the flesh. The gills are whitish. The stem is thin and viscous, often lemon yellow.

GROWING SEASON: summer – autumn

HABITAT: rotting wood, deciduous and coniferous

FREQUENCY: common

EDIBILITY: not worth picking

Agaricales

Tricholomataceae

Mycena haematopus (x 3.7)

The campanulate cap is pinky-brown. If the stem is damaged it exudes a brownish-red milk. Grows in clumps.

GROWING SEASON: summer – autumn

HABITAT: dead broad-leaved trees

FREQUENCY: fairly common

EDIBILITY: not worth picking

Tricholomataceae

Mycena seynesii (x 1.3)

The habitat helps to identify this Mycena. The pinkish-brown, smooth, campanulate cap is up to 4 cm (2½ in) in diameter. The pinkish gills are clearly edged in purple-brown. The smooth stem is the same colour as the cap.

GROWING SEASON: summer – autumn

HABITAT: on pine cones

FREQUENCY: fairly common

EDIBILITY: not worth picking

Entolomataceae

Entoloma sinuatum (x 1)

Syn.: *Entoloma lividum*. The Livid Entoloma is a fleshy species which often grows in rings consisting of numerous specimens. The cap is yellowish-white to silver-grey and striped to some extent. The thickish stem is whitish. The gills are yellow at first, then turn pink as the spores ripen. The firm, white flesh gives off a strong smell of flour.

GROWING SEASON: summer – autumn

HABITAT: broad-leaved woods

FREQUENCY: fairly common

EDIBILITY: poisonous

Agaricales

Cortinariaceae

Cortinarius bulliardii (x 1.5)

Bulliard's Cortinarius has a smooth cap which grows to a maximum of 8 cm (3 in) in diameter. It is dark brown but pales to beige in dry weather. The violet gills become rust-coloured when mature. This Cortinarius would be unremarkable were it not for the bright red base of the stem, a feature which makes it very easy to recognise.

GROWING SEASON: autumn

HABITAT: broad-leaved trees

FREQUENCY: quite rare

EDIBILITY: not worth picking

Cortinariaceae

Cortinarius herculeus

This large Cortinarius, whose cap can easily attain 20 cm (8 in) in diameter, can be spotted even with closed eyes due to its very strong earthy odour which some people identify as smelling like DDT. The smell is particularly powerful in an enclosed space. This fungus only grows beneath cedars with which it forms a symbiotic association. The cap is reddish-brown, and is often decorated on the margin with the whitish remains of the veil. The white gills brown on maturity. The whitish foot is ringed with circlets of scales.

GROWING SEASON: autumn

HABITAT: cedar trees

FREQUENCY: quite rare

EDIBILITY: not worth picking

Cortinariaceae
Cortinarius semisanguineus (x 4.9)
The Semi-sanguine Cortinarius owes its name to its blood-red gills which contrast well with the brownish-fawn to yellow-olivaceous, fibrillose cap and tall, thin yellow stem which is sometimes a reddish colour at the base. The yellow flesh smells of radishes. The Sanguine Cortinarius (*Cortinarius sanguineus*) is entirely blood-red. These species are suspect.

GROWING SEASON: summer – autumn
HABITAT: especially conifers
FREQUENCY: fairly common
EDIBILITY: not worth picking

ABOVE

Cortinariaceae
Cortinarius orellanus (x 1.7)
The Annatto-coloured Cortinarius has a bright reddish-orange cap 3 – 8 cm (1 – 3 in) in diameter, covered in velvety fibrils. The gills are bright fawn-orange, turning rust-red when covered in ripe spores. The stem is fibrillose, golden-fawn washed with orange. The flesh is pale yellowish-red and smells of radishes. The common name derives from the general colouring which is similar to the orange food colouring derived from the Amazonian annatto tree (*Bixa orellana*), discovered by Francisco De Orellana.

GROWING SEASON: summer – autumn
HABITAT: broad-leaved (esp. oak trees)
FREQUENCY: fairly common
EDIBILITY: deadly poisonous

ABOVE

Cortinariaceae
Cortinarius rufoolivaceus (x 1)
A handsome species, typified by a coppery-red, viscous cap 10 cm (4 in) in diameter, paling to mauve at the margin. The stem is mauve at the top and yellowish-green below. The bulbous base is the same colour as the cap with olive-coloured gills which may be bluish. The white to mauvish flesh, which turns red at the bulb, is bitter.

GROWING SEASON: summer – autumn
HABITAT: broad-leaved trees in chalky soil
FREQUENCY: fairly common
EDIBILITY: not worth picking

Cortinariaceae

Inocybe calamistrata (x 5.9)

This Inocybe is rather unremarkable-looking with its strongly fibrillose, dark brown, hairy cap less than 5 cm (2 in) in diameter and brown gills. However, a surprise is in store for anyone who picks it, since it will reveal that its dark brown, hairy stem is a startling blue-green colour at the base, making it very easy to identify.

GROWING SEASON: summer – autumn

HABITAT: under trees

FREQUENCY: quite rare

EDIBILITY: not worth picking

ABOVE

Cortinariaceae

Cortinarius trivialis (x 1)

The Trivial Cortinarius belongs to the group of Cortinarius species with a viscous cap and stem. The olive-brown cap which is about 10 cm (4 in) in diameter is very glutinous. The stem is unusual, in that it is ringed with a set of gelatinous bracelets in sharp relief, all the way up the base to the cortina. The gills may be whitish or clearly violet but darken as the spores ripen.

GROWING SEASON: summer – autumn

HABITAT: broad-leaved trees

FREQUENCY: fairly common

EDIBILITY: not worth picking

OPPOSITE

Cortinariaceae

Galerina marginata (x 3)

This fungus is very variable in size. The smooth, reddish-fawn cap can grow to 7 cm (3 in) in diameter, and turns yellow as it dries out. The gills are cinnamon-coloured. The reddish stem is decorated with a small ring. The flesh smells and tastes of flour. The very similar *Galerina automnalis*, which is also deadly poisonous, has a grey, viscous cap. There is danger of possible confusion between this fungus and the Changing Pholiota (*Kuehneromyces mutabilis*) which is edible with a pleasant smell, and whose stem is covered with small scales below the ring.

GROWING SEASON: summer – autumn

HABITAT: on wood, especially conifers,
possibly on broad-leaved trees

FREQUENCY: fairly common

EDIBILITY: deadly poisonous

Strophariaceae

Stropharia aeruginosa (x 2.4)

The Verdigris Agaric has a viscous, blue-green cap which yellows with age. Young specimens have white tufts beneath the slime of the cap. When mature, the dark reddish-brown gills with whitish edges contrast with the pale blue-green stem which is covered in white tufts.

GROWING SEASON: summer – autumn

HABITAT: forests

FREQUENCY: fairly common

EDIBILITY: not worth picking

ABOVE

Strophariaceae

Hypholoma sublateritium (x 0.9)

Brick Caps is another species which grows in clumps. The specimens have fleshy, brick-red caps which may be 12 – 15 cm (5 – 6 in) in diameter, with a paler edge. The gills are yellow initially, darkening to olivaceous grey-brown. The reddish-yellow stem is solid with a veil which is almost a ring. The yellowish flesh is bitter.

GROWING SEASON: summer – autumn

HABITAT: on all types of wood

FREQUENCY: fairly common

EDIBILITY: not worth picking

ABOVE

Strophariaceae

Panaeolus sphinctrinus (x 1.55)

The conical, dark grey-brown cap which pales with age has a margin crenellated by the remains of the whitish veil. The gills are covered in alternating black and grey patches, sometimes described as cloudy.

GROWING SEASON: spring – summer – autumn

HABITAT: cowpats, dung

FREQUENCY: fairly common

EDIBILITY: poisonous

Fungi

Strophariaceae

Pholiota highlandensis (x 1.1)

Syn.: *Pholiota carbonaria*. The Carbon Pholiota grows only on burnt ground. The reddish-brown cap is covered in a shiny, slimy cuticle which peels away easily. The pale yellow gills turn brown as the spores mature. The pale yellow stem is fibrilose and squamose below the ring.

GROWING SEASON: summer – autumn – winter

HABITAT: burnt ground

FREQUENCY: common

EDIBILITY: not worth picking

Coprinaceae
Psathyrella lacrymabunda (x 1.6)
Syn.: *Lacrymaria lacrymabunda.* The
Weeping Psathyrella has an ochraceous-
brown cap covered in woolly fibrils which
wither with age. The dark gills are spotted.
The whitish stem is covered with a cortina.
There are fibrils at the base which blacken
when covered with spores.

GROWING SEASON: summer – autumn
HABITAT: woods, wasteland,
roadsides
FREQUENCY: fairly common
EDIBILITY: edible

BELOW

Amanitaceae
Amanita citrina (x 1.1)
The False Death Cap has a cap dotted with
flecks of white which varies in colour from
lemon to greenish-yellow. The margin is
smooth. The lemon to white stem has a
membranous ring. The bulbous base has
an edge. The flesh smells of radishes or
potatoes. The unpleasant taste and close
resemblance to the Death Cap are good
reasons not to pick it for eating.

GROWING SEASON: summer – autumn
HABITAT: woodland
FREQUENCY: common
EDIBILITY: not worth picking

FACING PAGE
Coprinaceae
Coprinus comatus (x 1.7)
Species of Coprinus are characterised by
the blackening and liquefaction of the
gills as the spores ripen, transforming
the fungus into a liquid mass, known as
deliquescence. They can only be picked
when very young and eaten on the same
day. The distinctive outline of the Shaggy
Ink Cap, which is 20 – 30 cm (8 – 12 in)
tall, is easy to recognise. The scaly cap
gives it its other common name, Lawyer's
Wig. The stem is longish and has a ring.

GROWING SEASON: almost year-round
HABITAT: grassland, wasteland
FREQUENCY: common
EDIBILITY: edible when young

Agaricales

Amanitaceae

Amanita muscaria (x 1.9 ; x 1.2 ; x 1.4)

The Fly Agaric is hard to miss with its large size and vermilion cap, dotted with white flecks. The gills and stem are also white. The stem has a membranous ring and a bulbous base, ringed with scaly folds. It is important to avoid confusion with the Amanita of the Caesars (*Amanita caesarea*), which does not grow as far north as the United Kingdom, and has a more orange-coloured cap, devoid of white patches, yellow gills and a yellow stem, the base of which is sheathed in a thick white volva.

GROWING SEASON: summer – autumn

HABITAT: birches or conifers (pines and spruces)

FREQUENCY: fairly common

EDIBILITY: poisonous

Amanitaceae

Amanita phalloides (x 2)

The Death Cap is responsible for most deaths by fungus poisoning in Europe. The most constant feature is that the base of the stem is enveloped in a white sac which is called the volva. Any unknown fungus should thus be carefully and completely unearthed from the soil. A smooth, pale yellow-green to olive-brown cap, slightly striated with darker lines, white gills with a greenish reflection, and a whitish-green variegated stem which may or may not have a membranous ring complete the portrait. There is a very similar entirely white form which is similar to the Spring Amanita (*Amanita verna*) and the Destroying Angel (*Amanita virosa*), both of which are also deadly poisonous.

GROWING SEASON: summer – autumn

HABITAT: woodland

FREQUENCY: fairly common

EDIBILITY: deadly poisonous

Agaricaceae

Macrolepiota rhacodes (x 2.9)

The cap of the Shaggy Parasol can grow to 15 cm (6 in) in diameter. The centre is smooth and brown, and tears progressively and concentrically into large brown scales on a cream background. The whitish gills are not attached to the tall rigid stem which ends in a bulb at the base. There is a membranous ring which is white initially, turning reddish-brown when bruised. The whitish flesh also soon turns orange-red. Specimens growing among rubble in parks or gardens should always be avoided since they are renowned for being a gastric irritant.

GROWING SEASON: summer – autumn

HABITAT: mostly under conifers

FREQUENCY: fairly common

EDIBILITY: risky to eat

Agaricaceae

Cystoderma carcharias (x 7)

This beautiful Cystoderma can be recognised by its pinkish-cream cap about 2 – 5 cm (1 – 2 in) in diameter. It is entirely covered with little granules which are clearly visible under a magnifying glass. The stem, which is the same colour as the cap, is enclosed in a granulose sheath opening out into a membranous ring. The gills are whitish. The fungus has a very unpleasant smell, which is often said to resemble DDT insecticide.

GROWING SEASON: summer – autumn

HABITAT: conifers

FREQUENCY: fairly common

EDIBILITY: not worth picking

ABOVE

Agaricaceae

Macrolepiota procera (x 0.9)

The Parasol Mushroom can be seen from far away, as the cap can be as big as 40 cm (16 in) across! It is covered in flaky scales which are a darker brown than the cap, except in the centre where there is a smooth disk. The rigid stem is covered with dark striations. It has a loose double ring. The flesh and gills are white. Only the cap can be eaten.

GROWING SEASON: summer – autumn

HABITAT: fields and clearings

FREQUENCY: fairly common

EDIBILITY: good to eat

ABOVE

Agaricaceae

Cystoderma terreyi (x 2)

The brick-red cap is densely covered with granulation. The gills are whitish. The pale reddish-orange stem is decorated with little whitish or reddish flakes or patches. The species can be clearly identified under the microscope by numerous very elongated cells on the gills, to which crystals are attached.

GROWING SEASON: summer – autumn

HABITAT: woodland

FREQUENCY: fairly rare

EDIBILITY: not worth picking

Fig.3

Cantharellaceae

The fungi in this group have a reproductive surface which is smooth or covered with veins or folds which may or may not be branched. This surface is covered by a cap which is carried on a stem. The fungi are funnel-shaped when the stem is full as in the Chanterelle (*Cantharellus cibarius*), and is in the shape of a hollow horn as in the Horn of Plenty (*Craterellus cornucopioides*). Many species make excellent eating and are readily identifiable due to the absence of gills under the cap which means that there can be no confusion with Agarics which they may superficially resemble (such as the Olive-tree Pleurotus). These fungi are also easy to pick, because when the weather is right, large groups of them (Yellow Chanterelle, Tubular Chanterelle, etc.) are to be found growing together.

FACING PAGE

Cantharellaceae

Cantharellus cibarius (x 4.3)

It is easy to find Chanterelles because their bright yellow colour is so eye-catching. To avoid any confusion with other species, such as the False Chanterelle (*Hygrophoropsis aurantiaca*), all that is needed is to check that the characteristic folds are on the underside of the cap. The False Chanterelle has a velvety cap and is a darker colour. The Olive-tree Pleurotus (*Omphalotus olearius*), which is similar but gilled, is poisonous.

GROWING SEASON: spring – summer – autumn

HABITAT: broad-leaved or coniferous woods

FREQUENCY: fairly common

EDIBILITY: excellent

Cantharellaceae

Cantharellus lutescens (x 2.2)

The Yellowing Chanterelle is easy to pick because it has the habit of growing in large colonies. The trumpet-shaped cap has an undulating edge tinged with grey and washed with orange. The colour contrasts strongly with the furrowed, hollow stem and with the wrinkled, veined hymenium*, both of which are orange. The flesh has quite an agreeable, fairly strong fruity smell.

GROWING SEASON: summer – autumn
HABITAT: woodland
FREQUENCY: fairly common
EDIBILITY: excellent

Cantharellaceae

Craterellus cornucopioides (x 3.7)

The Horn of Plenty has the unfortunate name of *Trompette des Morts* (Trumpet of the Dead) in French, no doubt due to its trumpet shape and overall dark colour. The English name is far more appropriate, since it is so good to eat. It is dark brown to black in colour and grows in large numbers. Some specimens can be as tall as 15 cm (6 in). The elastic flesh is easy to dry which means it can be eaten at a later date. The only possible confusion could be with other species of Chanterelle which are similar in colour, so there is no danger of poisoning, since all these species are edible.

GROWING SEASON: summer – autumn
HABITAT: mainly broad-leaved trees
FREQUENCY: fairly common
EDIBILITY: excellent

Fig.4

Clavariaceae

Typical specimens of this family look like coral, hence the name Coral Fungi. The fruiting body consists of a stem which splits into branches, the reproductive organs covering the surface of these branches. The consistency may be coriaceous or fragile. The branches are generally cylindrical but may also be flattened, the whole looking something like a cauliflower. The species are identified by the habitat, shape and colour, and sometimes by smell. However, a microscope is often needed as many of the Coral Fungi resemble each other closely, particularly the yellow Clavarias. This group also includes the so-called Club Fungi, which look like a single upright stalk of very variable size, thread-like in species of Typhula or thickened into a club shape in the Giant Fairy Club (*Clavariadelphus pistillaris*).

FACING

Clavariaceae

Clavulinopsis corniculata (x 7)

The Stag-horn Fungus can grow to 10 cm (4 in). The slender stem divides into branches, each of which produces two more crescent-shaped branches at the tip, like the antlers of a stag. The whole fungus is egg-yellow in colour. The very firm flesh emits a floury smell when broken.

GROWING SEASON: autumn

HABITAT: meadows, lawns, clearings or moss

FREQUENCY: quite rare

EDIBILITY: not worth picking

Pterulaceae

Pterula multifida (x 3.6)

This species grows in clumps of clustered, very thin, sinuous, tapering branches which have a rather elastic consistency. They are whitish at the tip and brown at the base.

GROWING SEASON: summer – autumn

HABITAT: conifers and
mixed woods

FREQUENCY: rather common

EDIBILITY: not worth picking

Clavariadelphaceae

Clavariadelphus pistillaris (x 3.7)

The Giant Fairy Club is very variable in height but can grow to 30 cm (12 in) and be 6 cm (2½ in) across. The fungus is distinguishable by its club-shaped tip which is convex and yellowish-brown. It stains brownish-violet when bruised, a reaction which is also reproduced in the flesh, which is white at first. The slightly bitter taste and spongy texture mean that it is by no means the most tasty of fungi. The closely related *Clavariadelphus truncatus* grows under conifers in the mountains. It has a flattened, truncated top and tastes rather sweetish.

GROWING SEASON: summer – autumn

HABITAT: broad-leaved trees

FREQUENCY: quite rare

EDIBILITY: not worth picking

Ramariaceae

Ramaria flavescens (x 1.4)

A large Clavaria (it can attain 20 cm/8 in in height) consisting of a thick, whitish trunk-like stem from which pale yellow to yellow-orange branches grow. They generally end in two to four points. The microscopic characteristics are useful to separate species with similar morphology. The consumer needs to avoid confusion with *Ramaria formosa* which has a laxative effect and whose branches are pink with yellow tips in the most typical specimens.

GROWING SEASON: summer – autumn

HABITAT: mixed woodland

FREQUENCY: fairly common

EDIBILITY: edible

Clavariaceae

Macrotyphula filiformis (x 2.6)

Syn.: *Macrotyphula juncea*. This Typhula is one of the largest in its group. It consists of long thread-like strands up to 15 cm (6 in) tall, at the base of which there is a cottony mycelium which sticks to the leaf on which it grows. It is similar in appearance to *Typhula phacorrhiza* which fruits on a lenticular mass (the sclerotium). Some similar species are difficult to spot since they are no larger than a couple of millimetres. It is not very appetizing.

GROWING SEASON: autumn

HABITAT: dead leaves

FREQUENCY: quite rare

EDIBILITY: not worth picking

Fig. 5

Hydnaceae

The only thing the members of this family of fungi have in common with each other is the reproductive organ which consists of a mass of tiny spines. The other characteristics (size, shape, texture, habitat, etc.) are very variable. Species that grow on the ground have a cap supported on a stem. The flesh of such fungi may be tender as in the Wood Hedgehog (*Hydnum repandum*) or of corky consistency such as *Calodon*. Species that grow on wood may have coriaceous flesh and a stem as in the Ear-pick Fungus (*Auriscalpium vulgare*). They may be attached directly to the growing medium and have soft flesh as in the edible *Hericium erinaceus*, or they may be coriaceous and look like Cup Fungi or Polypores depending on how the cap develops (*Climacodon septentrionalis*).

OPPOSITE AND PAGE **74**

Hydnaceae

Hydnum repandum (x 3.7; x 2)

The Wood Hedgehog is easily recognisable by its fleshy, ochre- to reddish-brown cap which may exceed 10 cm (4 in) in diameter. It is irregular, lobed and may be smooth or slightly velvety. The underside is covered with a mass of tiny spines which are paler in colour than the cap. The flesh is slightly fibrous so younger specimens are much better for eating. It often grows in fairy rings. There is a smaller, redder variety and another which is completely white.

GROWING SEASON: summer – autumn

HABITAT: broad-leaved trees or conifers

FREQUENCY: common

EDIBILITY: good to eat

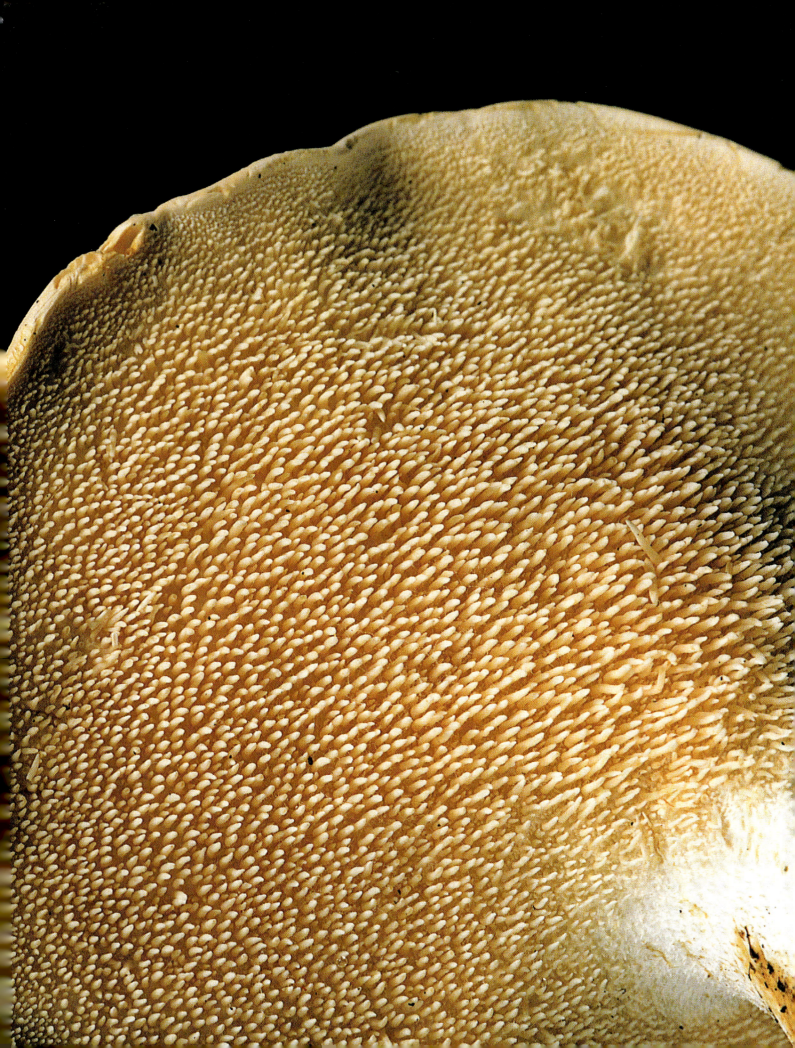

Auriscalpiaceae

Auriscalpium vulgare (x 6.8)

This curious fungus is always of interest because it looks so unusual. The Ear-pick Fungus has a brown, kidney-shaped cap about 2 cm (1 in) in diameter. It is covered in short, rough hairs. The cap is borne on a long, brown lateral stem which is also hairy. The hymenium consists of little whitish-grey spines, darkening to brown. The whole fungus darkens with age.

GROWING SEASON: almost year round, if the weather conditions are suitable

HABITAT: pine cones embedded in humus

FREQUENCY: fairly common

EDIBILITY: not worth picking

Polyporaceae

Polypores usually have no stem and grow mostly on wood. The flesh is usually leathery. The reproductive area may be poraceous, as in the boletes, or gilled as in the agarics, and very occasionally consists of spines. A few species which grow on the ground and have a stem also have pores, so are reminiscent of boletes, but the flesh is much more leathery and the tubes cannot be separated from the cap. The flesh may even have a corky consistency (as in the case of the Razor-strop Fungus) which explains why some polypores last for years. They are often spectacular in appearance and extremely large (they can weigh several kilograms). Polypores are notorious for the damage they do to the wood on which they grow, as they often cause wood-rot.

FACING PAGE

Coriolaceae

Trametes versicolor (x 2.3)

This polypore can be recognised by its kidney-shaped, concentric layers which are no thicker than 5 mm (¼ in) at the point at which they enter the wood. The cap is ringed with concentric, multicoloured bands which are alternately smooth and hairy. The pores are whitish-yellow and the whitish flesh is coriaceous. The fungus usually grows in large colonies.

GROWING SEASON: all year round

HABITAT: on any type of wood

FREQUENCY: very common

EDIBILITY: not worth picking

Fistulinaceae

Fistulina hepatica (x 2)

The Beefsteak Fungus at first resembles a small pink lump, but later extends out until it resembles a gelatinous tongue. The cap is 10 – 20 cm (4 – 8 in) long, orange-red to orange-brown and covered with little warts which look like papillae. As soon as it is touched, the fungus stains darker red. The underside of the cap consists of red tubes which are separate from each other, and which also turn red.

GROWING SEASON: summer – autumn
HABITAT: oak or chestnut stumps and trunks
FREQUENCY: quite common
EDIBILITY: edible, even when raw

Coriolaceae

Grifola frondosa (x 1.3)

The photograph shows a cultivated variety. This polypore, which grows at the base of tree trunks, consists of a cluster of little leaf-shaped or fan-shaped caps, radially furrowed and joined at a single lateral stem. The whole fruiting body may attain 50 cm (20 in) in diameter. The pores are whitish.

GROWING SEASON: summer – autumn
HABITAT: on stumps and base of trunks of broad-leaved trees
FREQUENCY: quite rare
EDIBILITY: edible

Coriolaceae

Daedaleopsis confragosa var. *tricolor* (x 3.7)

The Blushing Bracket spreads its fan-shaped or kidney-shaped brackets, which are about 10 cm (4 in) in diameter, on tree trunks or branches. The reddish-brown brackets are smooth, ridged and marked with darker concentric bands. The flesh is cream to reddish-brown. The underside consists of forked gills. Specimens with a porous underside belong to the *confragosa* variety.

GROWING SEASON: all year round
HABITAT: deciduous dead wood
FREQUENCY: fairly common
EDIBILITY: not worth picking

Coriolaceae

Hexagonia nitida (x 5.1)

This fungus forms tough hemispherical brackets 5 – 15 cm (2 – 6 in) in diameter. The cap is often striated with concentric bands and varies from brown to black, depending on the age. The wide pores are polygonal like a bees' nest.

GROWING SEASON: all year round

HABITAT: mainly on holm-oaks

FREQUENCY: fairly common on Mediterranean and warm Atlantic coasts

EDIBILITY: not worth picking

Coriolaceae

Piptoporus betulinus (x 0.75)

The Birch Polypore restricts itself to one host. It can reach 20 – 30 cm (8 – 12 in) in diameter, and forms a hoof-shaped excrescence, with a fatter margin. It is fixed to the substrate by the top of the cap. The cuticle is grey-brown, separable and cracks on maturity. The very small pores are whitish in colour. Although easy to find, the Birch Polypore is not worth eating.

GROWING SEASON: summer – autumn

HABITAT: on birch trees

FREQUENCY: common

EDIBILITY: not worth picking

Polyporaceae

Coriolaceae

Pycnoporus cinnabarinus

This distinctive polypore, which is 10 cm (4 in) in diameter, colonises tree trunks and branches, stumps or cut wood. It is easy to identify because it is bright vermilion red all over, darker in the pore area. This fungus has been used as a fabric dye.

GROWING SEASON: summer – autumn

HABITAT: especially on broad-leaved wood, rarely on conifers

FREQUENCY: uncommon

EDIBILITY: not worth picking

Schizophyllaceae

Schizophyllum commune (x 3.6)

The cap of this greyish-brown fungus is only 1 – 3 cm (⅛ – 1 in) in diameter, and has a woolly appearance. The pinkish gills are arranged in a fan shape and split lengthways. The texture is elastic in wet weather, tough and friable in dry weather.

GROWING SEASON: all year round

HABITAT: on all types of wood

FREQUENCY: very common

EDIBILITY: not worth picking

Ganodermataceae

Ganoderma lucidum (x 4.6)

The oval cap and lateral stem of the Lacquered Bracket are covered by a glossy, resinous layer that is mahogany to reddish-brown in colour. The white pores turn brown with age.

GROWING SEASON: summer – autumn

HABITAT: on stumps and trunks of broad-leaved trees

FREQUENCY: common

EDIBILITY: not worth picking

Corticalaceae

These fungi spread like a thin crust over the surface of wood and their reproductive surface is usually smooth, or virtually so. They may be of a cottony, floury, waxy, leathery or cornate consistency. Some species detach themselves from the substrate and form a cap or display a folded, dentate and almost poraceous reproductive surface, similar to that of polypores. Like polypores, they help to break down wood. Their thin fruiting bodies enable them to cover large areas and they are capable of doing a lot of damage. Dry Rot (*Merulius lacrymans*) is the best example. This fungus invades and destroys all types of woodwork, eating away at timber frames, joists and floorboards in damp houses. It can cause whole houses to collapse, injuring the inhabitants! In extreme cases, the only truly effective way of getting rid of this invasive parasite is to destroy the building itself!

FACING PAGE

Corticalaceae

Pulcherricium caeruleum (x 4.6)

This fungus creeps over surfaces in the form of a smooth or knobbly crust about 0.5 mm (⅙₆ inch) thick which can extend over a wide area. The dark blue colour, which is intense when the fungus is fresh, makes it very easy to identify on tree trunks or branches.

GROWING SEASON: all year round

HABITAT: on broad-leaved trees

FREQUENCY: fairly rare

EDIBILITY: not worth picking

Fig. 7

Fig.8

Gasteromycetes

This group contains about 1,000 species. It includes all fungi whose fertile part is initially enclosed in one or more cavities. On maturity, the device opens to the air in order to release the spores, using various dispersal systems which vary according to the fungus in question. The most standard shape consists of a rounded part which may or may not have a stem, and which releases a cloud of powdery spores (examples are puffballs, stalked puffballs and earth-balls). The fungus can emerge from an 'egg' and form a fruiting body of various shapes (as in the stinkhorns, earth-stars, and cage fungi). This is often on the outside or inside with a gelatinous substance which often has a nauseating smell and contains the spores (as in the case of the stinkhorns, dog stinkhorns and cage fungi). Or it may look like a bird's nest from which little round spore-filled sacs, called peridioles, are expelled (as in the various species of *Crucibulum*). Finally, this group contains species which live entirely underground. These tubercules become gelatinous or deliquescent as in the case of *Gautieria* species.

FACING PAGE

Clathraceae
Clathrus ruber (x 2.8)

This appears first as a whitish egg which opens, releasing a fragile coral red cage-like structure, the interior of which is covered with the gleba, a fœtid, olive-green, spore-bearing substance designed to attract insects. If the egg produces a sort of earth-star this is a similar species, *Anthurus archeri*. The closely related Stinkhorn (*Phallus impudicus*) is much more common.

GROWING SEASON: summer – autumn
HABITAT: gardens, parks, warm forests
FREQUENCY: fairly rare
EDIBILITY: not worth picking

ABOVE

Astraeaceae

Astraeus hygrometricus (x 1.7)

A typical fungus of sandy open spaces which owes its Latin name to the fact that it changes shape depending on the dryness of the weather conditions. When the weather is wet, the fungus opens into an earth-star about 5 cm (2 in) in diameter, dark brown in colour, the points of the star covered in a whitish fugaceous film. The round endoperidium in the centre tears open when the fungus is mature, releasing a cloud of brownish spores. When the weather is dry, the points fold into a ball around the endoperidium. The opening and closing of the points can be witnessed 'live' as the process takes only a few minutes, if the fungus is wetted or dried.

GROWING SEASON: all year round
HABITAT: dry places, especially sandy soil
FREQUENCY: fairly common in its habitat
EDIBILITY: not worth picking

ABOVE

Nidulariaceae

Crucibulum laeve (x 5.5)

The Bird's Nest Fungus has an extraordinary shape, in that it looks like a tiny cup only 1 cm (¼ in) in diameter at most. It grows on rotten wood. At first it is covered with a yellow-orange membrane which opens at the top, showing the tiny yellowish-cream button-shaped peridioles which contain the spores.

GROWING SEASON: summer – autumn
HABITAT: on rotten vegetation
FREQUENCY: common
EDIBILITY: not worth picking

FACING PAGE

Lycoperdaceae

Langermannia gigantea (x 0.9)

The Puffball is a large whitish mass which can reach 50 cm (20 in) in diameter and weigh several kilograms. The surface may be smooth or suede-like. The interior – known as the gleba – is soft and whitish. When mature, it becomes olive-brown and powdery and the external envelope tears to release the spores.

GROWING SEASON: summer – autumn
HABITAT: fields and grassland
FREQUENCY: quite rare
EDIBILITY: edible when young

Fungi

Lycoperdaceae

Lycoperdon perlatum (x 4.6)

The Pearly Puffball is club-shaped and grows to up to 8 cm (3 in) in height. The round, whitish head is supported on a stem of the same colour. The surface is sprinkled with conical, flattened spines or warts. The fungus turns brown with age and loses its warts, leaving a network of scars. A hole opens in the top from which a cloud of spores emerges. The Pearly Puffball can only be eaten as long as the flesh (or gleba) remains white and firm.

GROWING SEASON: summer – autumn

HABITAT: on the ground in coniferous or broad-leaved woods

FREQUENCY: common

EDIBILITY: edible when young

ABOVE

Mycenastraceae

Mycenastrum corium (x 0.7)

This puffball is more than 10 cm (4 in) in diameter. It is whitish at first, then turning grey and finally dark brown. It is characterised by an external thick, rigid covering which tears at the top of the star-shaped lobes, releasing the brown spores.

GROWING SEASON: autumn – winter

HABITAT: dry, sandy places, waste ground

FREQUENCY: rare

EDIBILITY: not worth picking

FACING

Tulostomataceae

Tulostoma brumale (x 3.1)

Stalked Puffballs are recognisable by their shape — a round head, perforated at the top, and a stem which is often buried. On maturity, the head releases a cloud of brown spores through the hole in the top which is known as an ostiole.

GROWING SEASON: autumn – winter

HABITAT: sandy, sunny places

FREQUENCY: fairly rare

EDIBILITY: not worth picking

Fig. 9

Heterobasidiomycetes

This group contains species which share microscopic characteristics, in that the cells on which the spores are borne are either septate* or of a special shape. To the naked eye, the most common of these fungi have shapes that are similar to those in the preceding groups but are gelatinous or leathery and grow on wood. For instance, the Yellow Staghorn Fungus (*Calocera viscosa*) looks like a Clavaria and the Jelly Tongue (*Pseudohydnum gelatinosum*) looks like a Hydnum. The Auricularia and Exidia genera are also gelatinous, but shrivel into a hard, dry lump in dry weather.

FACING PAGE

Auriculariaceae

Auricularia auricula-judae (x 4.6)

The Jew's Ear derives its name from the cup-shaped form with its ear-like lobes and circumvolutions. It has a soft and elastic consistency. The hymenium is purplish red-brown with a paler exterior. Specimens can exceed 10 cm (4 in) in diameter and colonies grow on trees. In dry weather, the Jew's Ear shrivels and hardens, swelling again as soon as it rains. It is especially valued as a food in China, where it is cultivated and thousands of tons are harvested.

GROWING SEASON: year round

HABITAT: on broad-leaved trees (maple, elder and Robinia trees)

FREQUENCY: depending on availability of the host

EDIBILITY: edible, even raw

Dacrymycetaceae

Calocera viscosa (x 4.3)

The Yellow Stagshorn Fungus looks like a tiny shrub as it only grows to a maximum of 10 cm (4 in) high. It is entirely bright orange. To avoid confusion with a Clavaria of a similar colour, you need only rub the branches between your fingers. The elastic, viscous texture will confirm the identification.

GROWING SEASON: summer – autumn

HABITAT: on rotten wood of conifers

FREQUENCY: common

EDIBILITY: not worth picking

ABOVE

Exidiaceae

Pseudohydnum gelatinosum (x 2.3)

The Jelly Tongue is attached to wood by a short lateral stem. It forms a kidney-shaped or spatulate bracket, the uppermost side of which is greyish at first, then grey-brown and dotted with hairs. The underside is covered in soft, translucent, whitish spines. The fungus is eaten raw in salads.

GROWING SEASON: summer – autumn

HABITAT: on wood, especially conifers

FREQUENCY: fairly common

EDIBILITY: edible, even raw

OPPOSITE

Tremellaceae

Tremella mesenterica (x 1)

The Yellow Brain Fungus is a golden-yellow gelatinous mass shaped like a brain or with foliate lobes about 5 – 10 cm (2 – 4 in) in size, attached to wood. In dry weather, it shrivels completely and forms into an almost invisible rubbery patch but swells up again as soon as it rains and returns to its original size.

GROWING SEASON: all year round

HABITAT: on deciduous wood

FREQUENCY: common

EDIBILITY: not worth picking

Dacrymycetaceae

Calocera viscosa (x 4.3)

The Yellow Stagshorn Fungus looks like a tiny shrub as it only grows to a maximum of 10 cm (4 in) high. It is entirely bright orange. To avoid confusion with a Clavaria of a similar colour, you need only rub the branches between your fingers. The elastic, viscous texture will confirm the identification.

GROWING SEASON: summer – autumn

HABITAT: on rotten wood of conifers

FREQUENCY: common

EDIBILITY: not worth picking

ABOVE

Exidiaceae

Pseudohydnum gelatinosum (x 2.3)

The Jelly Tongue is attached to wood by a short lateral stem. It forms a kidney-shaped or spatulate bracket, the uppermost side of which is greyish at first, then grey-brown and dotted with hairs. The underside is covered in soft, translucent, whitish spines. The fungus is eaten raw in salads.

GROWING SEASON: summer – autumn

HABITAT: on wood, especially conifers

FREQUENCY: fairly common

EDIBILITY: edible, even raw

OPPOSITE

Tremellaceae

Tremella mesenterica (x 1)

The Yellow Brain Fungus is a golden-yellow gelatinous mass shaped like a brain or with foliate lobes about 5 – 10 cm (2 – 4 in) in size, attached to wood. In dry weather, it shrivels completely and forms into an almost invisible rubbery patch but swells up again as soon as it rains and returns to its original size.

GROWING SEASON: all year round

HABITAT: on deciduous wood

FREQUENCY: common

EDIBILITY: not worth picking

Fungi

Fig. 10

Discomycetes

Under the microscope, these fungi are characterised by their spores which until maturity are contained in sacs called asci. The Cup Fungi (Pezizas) and fungi shaped like cushions or discs are in this category, whether they grow on the ground or on wood and whether or not they have a stem. The other characteristics are very variable, such as size, which ranges from a few millimetres to a few centimetres, colour (which may be yellow, red, green or violet) and texture, which may be glabrous or velvety. Certain fungi which have the traditional shape of a cap supported by a stem are also in this family. The cap may be spongy, as in the case of the Morels, have brain-like convolutions as in the case of the Gyromitras or be folded as in the Helvellas. The simplest have a head that is smooth and almost club-like in shape like the Fairy Clubs (these include the genera Mitrula, Spathularia and Leotia). Some Discomycetes live their whole life-cycle underground and look like tubercules (as in the case of the Black Périgord Truffle and the White Truffle).

FACING PAGE

Otideaceae

Aleuria splendens (x 9.1)

This Cup Fungus is identifiable from its yellow to orange inner surface. Under the microscope, its spores are surprisingly oval and are covered with a honeycomb network. The similar Orange Peel Fungus (*Aleuria aurantia*) is distinguished by its larger size and absence of a stem. The species grows in groups of several individuals, sometimes in clumps.

GROWING SEASON: summer – autumn

HABITAT: broad-leaved trees

FREQUENCY: rare

EDIBILITY: not worth picking

Helvellaceae

Gyromitra infula (x 1.8)

Gyromitras are recognisable by the cap which is distinct from the stem, and which consists of an outcrop of thick, deeply furrowed folds looking like the convolutions of a brain. This species is distinguished by its dark reddish-brown cap which is subdivided into several lobes, arranged in the form of a saddle or a hood. The size and complexity of the arrangement, which can exceed 20 cm (8 in) in height, makes the cap very fragile and breakable.

GROWING SEASON: summer – autumn
HABITAT: especially in the mountains
FREQUENCY: rare
EDIBILITY: poisonous

FACING

Morchellaceae

Morchella conica (x 1)

The Conical Morel darkens with age. The ribs of the cap run vertically from tip to base and are joined to each other by short,

transversal ridges to make a pattern of depressions. The whitish stem is as thick as the cap.

GROWING SEASON: spring
HABITAT: mostly under conifers
FREQUENCY: variable, depending on weather
EDIBILITY: excellent, but must be cooked

OPPOSITE

Morchellaceae

Verpa conica (x 1.9)

The Thimble Fungus has an ochraceous-brown to reddish-brown thimble-shaped cap which may be smooth or slightly wrinkled. The stem is hollow, ochraceous-white, and flecked with minute reddish marks. The whole fungus is very fragile and breakable.

GROWING SEASON: spring
HABITAT: beside waterways, damp places
FREQUENCY: uncommon
EDIBILITY: not worth picking

Fungi

Helvellaceae

Helvella crispa (x 2.3)

The White Helvella is notable for its white cap shaped like undulating, folded lobes and carried on a whitish stem which is furrowed, fluted and hollow. The species may attain 15 cm (6 in) in height; it is frequently found in forest clearings and alongside footpaths in the spring. Although poisonous when raw, the White Helvella is edible if well cooked and eaten in small quantities.

GROWING SEASON: spring – autumn – winter (depending on variety)

HABITAT: mainly broad-leaves

FREQUENCY: common

EDIBILITY: edible but risky

Helvellaceae

Helvella spadicea (x 5.9)

Syn.: *Helvella monachella*. This Helvella is typified by a saddle-shaped black cap on a smooth, white stem. The same edibility warnings apply as for *Helvella crispa*, namely that it must be well cooked.

GROWING SEASON: spring

HABITAT: sandy soil, heathland or farmland, beside water

FREQUENCY: fairly common

EDIBILITY: edible but risky

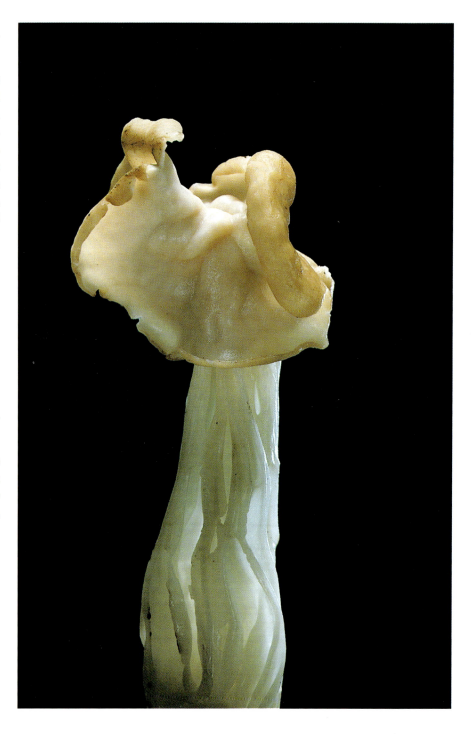

Sarcoscyphaceae

Sarcoscypha coccinea (x 7)

The Scarlet Elf Cup appears at a season when fungi are rare; its brilliant red colour contrasts with the surrounding wintry landscape. It is shaped like a cup 1 – 5 cm (½ – 2 in) in diameter, and grows on rotten branches and dead wood on the ground. The interior is smooth and bright scarlet, the matt exterior is pinkish-white.

GROWING SEASON: winter
HABITAT: on deciduous dead-
wood
FREQUENCY: quite rare
EDIBILITY: not worth picking

Otideaceae

Scutellinia scutellata (x 12)

This Cup Fungus looks like a tiny bright red plate; it reaches a maximum of 2 cm (¾ in) in diameter. The edge is fringed with short brown hairs. The numerous sub-species can only be identified with the help of a microscope.

GROWING SEASON: almost year round,
weather permitting
HABITAT: on deciduous deadwood, sometimes on
the ground
FREQUENCY: fairly common
EDIBILITY: not worth picking

Otideaceae

Otidea umbrina (x 3.1)

Syn.: *Otidea bufonia.* This fungus is about 5 cm (2 in) in diameter and is cup-shaped with wavy edges and split down one side to the base. The interior is dark brown, and the outside is slightly paler.

GROWING SEASON: summer – autumn
HABITAT: mixed woods
FREQUENCY: fairly common
EDIBILITY: not worth picking

Sarcoscyphaceae

Sarcoscypha coccinea (x 7)

The Scarlet Elf Cup appears at a season when fungi are rare; its brilliant red colour contrasts with the surrounding wintry landscape. It is shaped like a cup 1 – 5 cm (½ – 2 in) in diameter, and grows on rotten branches and dead wood on the ground. The interior is smooth and bright scarlet, the matt exterior is pinkish-white.

GROWING SEASON: winter

HABITAT: on deciduous deadwood

FREQUENCY: quite rare

EDIBILITY: not worth picking

Otideaceae

Scutellinia scutellata (x 12)

This Cup Fungus looks like a tiny bright red plate; it reaches a maximum of 2 cm (¾ in) in diameter. The edge is fringed with short brown hairs. The numerous sub-species can only be identified with the help of a microscope.

GROWING SEASON: almost year round, weather permitting

HABITAT: on deciduous deadwood, sometimes on the ground

FREQUENCY: fairly common

EDIBILITY: not worth picking

Otideaceae

Otidea umbrina (x 3.1)

Syn.: *Otidea bufonia.* This fungus is about 5 cm (2 in) in diameter and is cup-shaped with wavy edges and split down one side to the base. The interior is dark brown, and the outside is slightly paler.

GROWING SEASON: summer – autumn

HABITAT: mixed woods

FREQUENCY: fairly common

EDIBILITY: not worth picking

Geoglossaceae

Microglossum viride (x 2.5)

In order to find the Green Earth-Tongue, you will need to search its habitat thoroughly – damp woods in autumn – among mosses or dead leaves. It has a fusiform head and is about 5 cm (2 in) tall. The olive to dark green head is compressed and furrowed vertically and is supported by a smooth stem of the same colour, all of which enables it to camouflage itself from the casual stroller. It is distinguished from *Leotia atrovirens*, which is shorter and thicker, has a gelatinous consistency and presents different characteristics under the microscope.

GROWING SEASON: autumn

HABITAT: damp forests

FREQUENCY: fairly rare

EDIBILITY: not worth picking

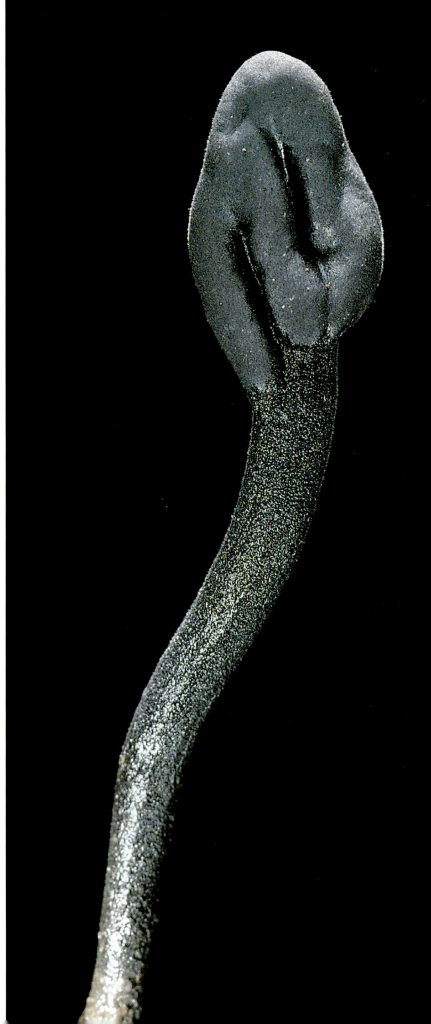

Geoglossaceae

Trichoglossum hirsutum (x 7.3)

The Earth Tongue is entirely black and can reach a height of 10 cm (4 in). The club-shaped head is compressed and furrowed lengthwise, a typical shape for Ascomycetes. However, it is difficult to distinguish between the various black species without the help of a microscope. Fortunately, a magnifying glass is useful in this case because it reveals that the fungus is covered with clearly visible hairs on the stem.

GROWING SEASON: summer – autumn

HABITAT: grassland,
marshes or sparse
woodland

FREQUENCY: fairly common

EDIBILITY: not worth picking

Leotiaceae

Leotia lubrica (x 8.2)

This remarkable Ascomycete has a rounded olive-yellow head with an inrolled margin, supported on a yellow stem. The fungus is gelatinous.

GROWING SEASON: summer – autumn

HABITAT: damp woods

FREQUENCY: fairly common

EDIBILITY: not worth picking

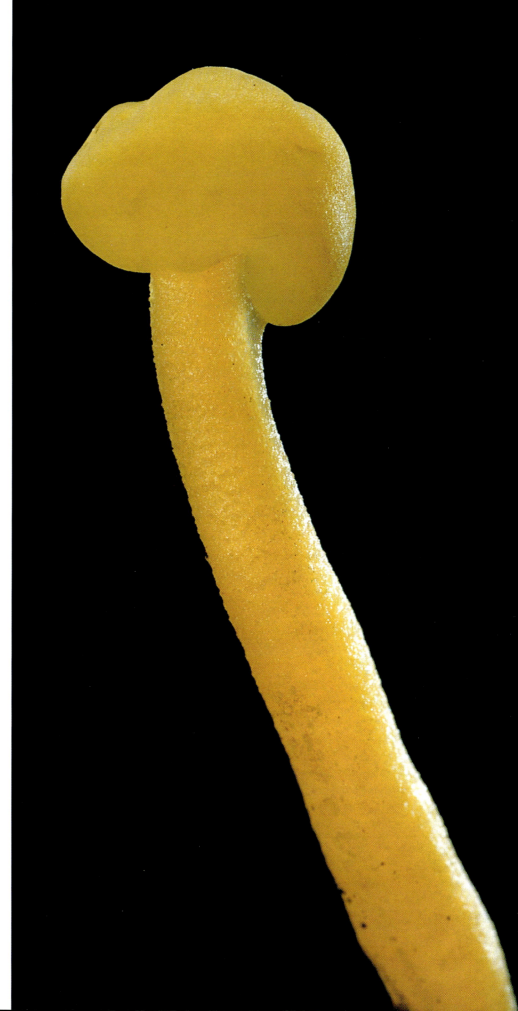

Helotiaceae

Ascocoryne sarcoides (x 5.5)

This Ascomycete grows in colonies of many specimens. When mature, it looks like a purple to pinkish-violet disc about 1 cm (½ in) diameter, often with a slight central depression, and fixed to the growing medium by a stem. A microscope is essential in order to be able to differentiate between this fungus and closely related species.

GROWING SEASON: autumn
HABITAT: damp forests
FREQUENCY: fairly rare
EDIBILITY: not worth picking

Tuberaceae

Tuber melanosporum (x 2; x 10.6)

The Black Truffle or 'Black Diamond' spends its entire life underground. It consists of a fleshy mass about 5 – 10 cm (2 – 4 in) in diameter, though a few species have been known to grow much larger (a few of them exceeding 1 kg/2½ lb in weight!). The flesh or gleba is white at first, then blackish, marbled with white veins when mature. The black exterior is covered with hexagonal warts. The Black Truffle has a strong, very pleasant smell, which is why it is such a delicacy.

GROWING SEASON: winter
HABITAT: especially under oak
FREQUENCY: rare
EDIBILITY: excellent

Discomycetes

Fig. 11

Pyrenomycetes

As in the case of the Discomycetes, the spores of the Flask Fungi are also contained inside asci or sacs. However, in this case the asci are themselves enclosed in a leathery or fleshy covering called a stroma. The Flask Fungi often parasitise plants, and this may have serious economic consequences (as in the case of Ergot (*Claviceps purpurea*)). A few species are common or remarkable, such as the species of Nectria which grow in large numbers on dead branches and look like tiny, red pustules; the Hypoxylons, leathery, black or brown crusts which spread over wood, the Xylarias, also on wood, which are black and rigid and are shaped similarly to Fairy Clubs; and the club-shaped Cordyceps which parasitises insects and subterranean fungi.

FACING PAGE

Xylariaceae

Hypoxylon fragiforme (x 2.7)

This fungus takes the form of a hard, hemispherical excrescence about 1 cm (½ in) in diameter, reddish-brown but blackening with age. Often irregular in shape, with warty skin, the fungus reveals little black boxes when cut: these are the peritheces which contain the spores.

GROWING SEASON: all year round

HABITAT: especially on dead beechwood

FREQUENCY: common

EDIBILITY: not worth picking

Fig. 11

Pyrenomycetes

As in the case of the Discomycetes, the spores of the Flask Fungi are also contained inside asci or sacs. However, in this case the asci are themselves enclosed in a leathery or fleshy covering called a stroma. The Flask Fungi often parasitise plants, and this may have serious economic consequences (as in the case of Ergot (*Claviceps purpurea*)). A few species are common or remarkable, such as the species of Nectria which grow in large numbers on dead branches and look like tiny, red pustules; the Hypoxylons, leathery, black or brown crusts which spread over wood, the Xylarias, also on wood, which are black and rigid and are shaped similarly to Fairy Clubs; and the club-shaped Cordyceps which parasitises insects and subterranean fungi.

FACING PAGE

Xylariaceae

Hypoxylon fragiforme (x 2.7)

This fungus takes the form of a hard, hemispherical excrescence about 1 cm (½ in) in diameter, reddish-brown but blackening with age. Often irregular in shape, with warty skin, the fungus reveals little black boxes when cut: these are the peritheces which contain the spores.

GROWING SEASON: all year round

HABITAT: especially on dead beechwood

FREQUENCY: common

EDIBILITY: not worth picking

LEFT-HAND PAGE, BOTTOM
AND ABOVE

Tuberaceae

Tuber melanosporum (x 2; x 10.6)

The Black Truffle or 'Black Diamond' spends its entire life underground. It consists of a fleshy mass about 5 – 10 cm (2 – 4 in) in diameter, though a few species have been known to grow much larger (a few of them exceeding 1 kg/2½ lb in weight!). The flesh or gleba is white at first, then blackish, marbled with white veins when mature. The black exterior is covered with hexagonal warts. The Black Truffle has a strong, very pleasant smell, which is why it is such a delicacy.

GROWING SEASON: winter

HABITAT: especially under oak

FREQUENCY: rare

EDIBILITY: excellent

Discomycetes

Diatrypaceae

Diatrype disciformis (x 2.7)

These tiny, black, almost circular discs, about 3 mm (⅒ in) in diameter, encrust the bark of dead wood, looking like a dark pustule outcrop. When cut open each disk is white, filled with black cells.

GROWING SEASON: all year round

HABITAT: mainly on beechwood

FREQUENCY: common

EDIBILITY: not worth picking

Xylariaceae

Xylaria hypoxylon (x 7.3)

The Candle-snuff Fungus looks like a snuffed-out candle or a tiny, leathery, leafless tree. The stem is hairy and black at the base. The branches are slightly flattened, white at first, then darkening.

GROWING SEASON: all year round

HABITAT: especially on broad-leaved wood

FREQUENCY: fairly common

EDIBILITY: not worth picking

Fig. 12

Myxomycetes

The Slime Fungi consist of about 700 species whose life-cycle contains a stage known as the 'plasmodium', in the course of which it is capable of moving in search of a suitable environment and the substrate needed for reproduction. During this mobile phase, the fungus feeds on diverse organic matter such as bacteria and moulds. As soon as conditions are favourable, the fungus attaches itself to a substrate and changes shape in order to produce a fruiting body. If conditions are adverse, it turns into a dense mass known as a scle-rotium. Some species, such as *Fuligo septica*, have a clearly visible plasmodium, but in most cases it is invisible and only the fruiting body, which is itself usually quite small, can be used for purposes of identification. The quest for Myxomycetes is thus the province of the enthusiast who, armed with a magnifying glass, knows how to explore a log, a pile of leaves or a tree trunk which from experi-ence they know to be a good place in which to find Slime Fungi.

PAGES 116–117

Trichiaceae

Trichia decipiens (x 13)

Even these immature fungi demonstrate the beauty of Myxomycetes. Each specimen, which attains about 2 or 3 mm (⅛ in) in height, looks like a sac on a stem. When ripe, it turns yellow and tears open to release the spores. The plasmodium is white or pink.

GROWING SEASON: all year round, weather permitting

HABITAT: damp spruce, on dead wood

FREQUENCY: fairly common

EDIBILITY: not worth picking

Lycogalaceae

Lycogala epidendron

This species resembles tiny balls or cushions about 1 cm (½ in) in diameter. At
first the specimens are soft and bright
pink, but they turn brown and eventually
black when their covering becomes thin
and breakable and finally breaks open,
releasing a cloud of spores. The plasmodium is coral red.

GROWING PERIOD: spring – summer –
autumn
HABITAT: on dead wood
FREQUENCY: fairly common
EDIBILITY: not worth picking

If you want a good harvest of fungi, it is vital to know the biotope and the sort of weather in which wild mushrooms grow. That type of knowledge can only be acquired over a number of years, but it means that you will have plenty to take home, as long as the habitat and season are right.

GROWING CONDITIONS

General Conditions

These depend on fungus type, which can be classified in three categories:
– leathery species whose fruiting bodies last all year round and which grow on wood (polypores, etc.)
– tiny, ephemeral fungi which grow in the soil, on wood or on dung almost all year round, as soon as there is any rain. They disappear very quickly as soon as it is windy or sunny (species of Marasmius, Coprinus, Mycena and the small Ascomycetes)
– most of the fleshy species which require plenty of water and warmth, and only appear for a limited time, at specific seasons. In the temperate zones of the northern hemisphere, the best times to find fungi are spring and autumn. However, if the summer is rainy or the winter mild, fungi may extend their growing season.
In spring, it is a good idea to look beside water, a habitat which Ascomycetes seem to favour. Summer favours spots which are frequently visited by storms and which are kept moist by showers. This means looking in meadows or sparse clumps of trees or in the mountains, where altitude and aspect play a part (the north face being cooler and wetter than the south face). In autumn, there is enough water everywhere and it is the drop in temperature which stops growth. As the season progresses, fungi can only be found at increasingly low altitudes, ending up by the sea in winter where the climate is generally more temperate, thus extending the growing season.

Local Conditions

The local vegetation also plays a vital role in changing growing conditions on a local level. For instance, a light and airy pine forest dries out more quickly than a dense plantation of fir trees.
The nature of the soil – whether it is limestone, chalk or clay – is also an important factor.
By making the soil dry out faster, the wind will prevent fruiting bodies from appearing or will accelerate the disappearance of those already above ground. In a single day, the wind can make even a large fleshy fungus unrecognisable.
Taking account of the relative importance of these various parameters, there are certain major ecological categories:
– open grassland (meadows, lawns)
– mountain plains whose vegetation is associated with dwarf trees
– places that are permanently wet or damp (marshes, swamps, peat bogs)
– cultivated land (farmland, greenhouses, flowerpots, etc.), notable for their constant change
– sand dunes by the sea
– carbonaceous environments (slag-heaps, charcoal heaps, burnt ground)
– forests, which are the favourite habitat for most species but in which it is often necessary to be able to recognise the host tree. Although it is easy to distinguish between coniferous and broad-leaved trees, it is also useful to be able to recognise the various species of tree so as to have a clear idea of the environment and thus be able to predict what kinds of fungi are likely to be found there.

WHAT THE ENTHUSIAST NEEDS TO KNOW

Fungus Forays

The commonest species are generally identified in their own habitat. However, in the case of rarer species, it is often necessary to pick samples and study them later. The picking and transport must therefore be performed carefully in order to keep the fungi as fresh as possible and avoid destroying very fragile characteristics which may be vital for identification purposes (such as the fugaceous ring of the Lepiotas and the powdery veil of the Coprinus species).

A fairly long-bladed, rigid knife will allow you to extract the whole fruiting body from the ground even when it is deeply buried in the ground or embedded in tree bark. For transport purposes, it is preferable to use a light plastic tool-box with many compartments, as it is light and impervious to damp, while making it possible to separate each species. Each specimen should be wrapped in newspaper which protects against shock and above all prevents the fungus from drying out too quickly. The smallest, most fragile fungi should be kept in the small plastic canisters used for storing photo film. It is quite important to gather various specimens of different ages for a single species because, like all living things, fungi change as they grow older. Agarics, for instance, whose gills may be white or very pale pink at first will darken almost to black and the brilliant blue gills of a Cortinarius may have turned dirty brown by the following day. These are just two examples. Climatic conditions are important because there may be desiccation, heavy rain or frost, all of which will affect the look of the fungi.

Nor should a pencil and notebook be forgotten, as the specific details which are likely to be needed for subsequent study should be noted down immediately. The ecology and such fugaceous characteristics as smell, texture and the colour in the hygrophanous* species which will change with the amount of water absorption all need recording. A magnifying glass with a magnification of at least six times is also useful to be able to see those elements which are hard to spot with the naked eye and which may escape notice later in artificial light (such as the coloured hairs on certain species of Mycena).

A few chemicals which will produce interesting colour reactions complete the field kit of the dedicated mycologist.

Identification

The best way is to use books which contain fungus identification keys. The key works as a sort of questionnaire in which the questions on the morphology of the fungi are in descending order of generality. At each step, the reader has a choice between two answers. Depending on which seems best to describe the specimen in question, you are directed to the subsequent stage where the process is repeated until you finally reach the stage which contains the name of the fungus. The following stage consists in checking whether the species described under the name which has been reached really does correspond to the specimen in question. The resemblance thus needs to be checked with the help of photos or coloured drawings and you also need to check that the descriptive text associated with the name obtained 'matches' the specimen collected.

An incorrect interpretation of the questionnaire or pictures may lead to the wrong results if there has been no prior attempt to recognise the characteristics which you should be looking for (learning to evaluate the viscosity of a species in dry weather, knowing how to identify certain smells, etc.). It is for this reason that the real enthusiast learns and completes his or her knowledge by joining a local organisation of experts, such as a mycological society, pharmacy faculty, etc. Through field trips, displays, advice sessions and expert explanations, he will gain experience it would be hard to get in any other way.

Examination with the naked eye is often not enough and a microscope is often required. This will make it possible to observe numerous additional characteristics, making identification more certain. Microscopic examination reveals the size, shape and colour of the cells, as well as other astonishing displays of natural phenomena which make the investigation a constant pleasure.

Collecting Fungi

The problem therefore arises of how best to preserve a fungus so that it can be studied at a later date. The preferred way to solve this problem is to dry the fungus and store it in a small labelled bag, away from light, humidity and insects. Although this procedure changes the external aspect of the fungus entirely, the microscopic characteristics remain observable, even after many years. In order to render as faithful an image of the specimen as possible, two additional techniques are available: drawing and photography. The first one has the advantage of producing a reliable result quickly, the second makes it possible to highlight certain details.

FUNGI FOR THE TABLE

Picking and Eating

Picking fungi for the purpose of eating them means having a (perfect!) knowledge of a rather restricted list of edible or poisonous species. When collecting fungi it is important to respect the natural surroundings. Do not destroy any species of fungi that you cannot identify or those known to be poisonous, because they are part of the diversity of the environment and play an important role in the life of the forest. They take part in the breakdown of organic material and facilitate the growth of trees by supplying them with nutrients while protecting their roots against pathogens.

Although it does not harm the mycelium when a whole fungus is removed, including the base, it is nevertheless preferable to slice it off at soil level, and above all to avoid tramping over and tamping down the substrate on which it grows. It is wisest to concentrate on the best-known species and those prized for their edibility. Do not pick excessive quantities. Here is a list of the best edible fungi: the Amanita of the Caesars (*Amanita caesarea*), the Blusher (*Amanita rubescens*), the Bay-capped Bolete (*Xerocomus badius*), Cep or Penny Bun Mushroom (*Boletus edulis*), Chanterelle (*Cantharellus cibarius*), Shaggy Ink Caps or Lawyer's Wig (*Coprinus comatus*), the Deceiver (*Laccaria laccata*), the Saffron Milk-cap (*Lactarius deliciosus*), the Parasol Mushroom (*Macrolepiota procera*), the Fairy Ring Champignon (*Marasmius oreades*), Morels (*Morchella* sp.), *Agrocybe aegerita*, the Wood Blewit (*Lepista nuda*), the Wood Hedgehog (*Hydnum repandum*), the Oyster Mushroom (*Pleurotus ostreatus*), the Field Mushroom (*Agaricus campestris*), *Russula mustelina*, the Charcoal Burner (*Russula cyanoxantha*), the Green Cracking Russula (*Russula virescens*), St George's Mushroom (*Calocybe gambosa*), the Equestrian Tricholoma (*Tricholoma equestre*), *Tricholoma portentosum*, *Tricholoma terreum*, the Horn of Plenty (*Craterellus cornucopioides*) and the Black Truffle (*Tuber melanosporum*).

Responsible ecological behaviour involves leaving doubtful fungi in their natural environment. When in doubt, it is preferable to pick only a few representative specimens of the species. They should be of different stages of growth, if possible, and

should be transported separately from the other fungi picked, wrapped in such a way as to retain their morphological characteristics. They may thus be presented in best condition to a pharmacist or the members of a mycological society who will be delighted to share their knowledge with the perplexed gatherer.

It is a good idea to check each fungus carefully when cleaning them, especially if several people have pooled their harvest; a dangerous intruder could easily be inserted into the crop.

FUNGI THROUGH THE YEAR

Winter

Although fleshy fungi are rarely to be found during cold spells, the leathery species which grow on wood are impervious to bad weather. One thus finds polypores such as the Hoof Fungus or Tinder Fungus (*Fomes fomentarius*), so-called because it is shaped like a horse's hoof, the inner part of which was used to staunch bleeding in surgery or as a firelighter, and *Trametes versicolor*, one of the commonest bracket fungi, whose multilobed cap is covered with concentric, shiny rings alternating with velvety, matt ones. There are also the fungi that spread like a thin crust over branches and tree trunks, such as *Pulcherricium caeruleum*, with its striking blue colour, or the Hairy Stereum (*Stereum hirsutum*), very common on dead wood, whose cap has a smooth, bright yellow-orange undersurface.

Fungi which may be encountered are:
– leathery species with gills, including *Schizophyllum commune*, whose woolly, whitish caps are split lengthwise, or the Maze-gill (*Daedalea quercina*) with their wide, labyrinthine gills
– gelatinous species, most frequently in their desiccated, invisible state, but which swell up again as soon as they are sufficiently waterlogged, such as Yellow Brain Fungus (*Tremella mesenterica*), a mass of bright yellow folds, or Witches' Butter (*Exidia glandulosa*), an ugly black mass.

Those fleshy fungi that are to be seen in the winter are usually small and are of no interest for eating purposes. They are represented mainly by a few species of Galera and similar genera, most of which are reddish-brown all over and hard to iden-

tify. There are also a few little late Clitocybe species and a few small Collybias which grow exclusively on pine and spruce cones buried in leaf litter.

Of the winter Ascomycetes, the most handsome is probably the Scarlet Elf Cap (*Sarcoscypha coccinea*), which grows in damp places on branches and twigs and attracts the eye thanks to a bright cup with a scarlet interior.

Gourmets can harvest the Velvet Shank (*Flammulina velutipes*) which grows in tufts on stumps and is recognisable by its slightly viscous orange cap and above all its handsome stem covered with tiny, thick hairs forming a velvety layer, and the Jew's Ear (*Auricularia auricula-judae*), an ear-shaped orange-brown excrescence of an elastic consistency in the fresh state, with a veined interior, which grows on broad-leaved trees, especially elder. And with luck, the dark brown, shell-shaped caps of the Oyster Mushroom (*Pleurotus ostreatus*), attached to tree trunks; but the prize of winter fungus forays is the Black Truffle (*Tuber melanosporum*), a black-brown lump covered with polygonal warts and with a strongly perfumed black flesh veined with white, reserved for the proud possessors of a truffle-hunting dog, because it grows underground.

Spring

MARCH–MAY

This is the season for many of the fleshy Ascomycetes, such as the Crown Elf Cap (*Sarcosphaera crassa*), which starts as a globule and bursts open into a violet star, emerging from the forest floor in pine and mixed woods. The Veined Elf Cap (*Disciotis venosa*) is a sort of large cup with many wrinkles and veins which smells strongly of bleach when broken and grows in sparsely wooded areas. This is also the season of the Helvellas and Gyromitras but especially of the Morels which grow in the mountains or on the plains under various types of tree, on farm waste as well as on burnt ground, depending on the species. When out rambling, you may encounter large, bright yellow clumps of Sulphur Tuft (*Hypholoma fasciculare*) whose gills are yellow at first, turning olive-green when ripe. The stem is cortinaceous* and the flesh is very bitter and thus inedible. Another spring species is *Clitocybe vermicularis*, a reddish-brown fungus which grows mainly under conifers, such as spruce and larch, and whose stem is extended by rhizomorphs (thick strands of mycelium which look like roots). A few Entolomas appear in the spring, notably *Entoloma clypeatum*, which smells strongly of flour and grows under fruit trees, rose bushes and hawthorn.

In addition to the highly-prized Morels, mushroom-eaters look for the March Hygrophorus (*Hygrophorus marzuolus*), which is well hidden under leaf-mould from beeches or conifers, and whose lubricated cap is white at first, darkening to black. The St George's Mushroom (*Calocybe gambosa*) is recognisable due to its squat shape, white to pale brown cap and compact flesh, as well as its strong floury smell. It grows in grassy places where it often forms fairy rings.

JUNE

The spring Ascomycetes give way to the earliest Amanitas, which are both poisonous species, the Jonquil Amanita (*Amanita gemmata*), an odourless species whose yellow cap is dotted with white patches, and the Spring Amanita (*Amanita verna*), which is pure white, with a ringed stem and sheathed volva*. A few Inocybes are also present, mainly the highly poisonous *Inocybe patouillardii*, one of the largest species in the genus. This fungus has a fibrillous cap which is white at first like the stem, reddening with age and which has a deceptively fruity odour. It is found under broad-leaved trees and in parks. A few Milk-caps are out (including *L. rufus* and *L. quietus*) but none of any interest for the table.

The mushroom-gatherer's basket may be filled with The Blusher (*Amanita rubescens*) which must be eaten cooked. The cap is usually reddish-brown covered with greying warts, the stem is bulbous and the ring is striated; the most typical feature is the way in which the flesh reddens when cut. There are also a few Russulas around, such as *Russula vesca*, whose cap is normally maroon to brown, and whose cuticle* often retracts at the margin*, revealing the cream-coloured gills, and the Charcoal Burner (*Russula cyanoxantha*), with its violet and green cap and its thick, white gills, which bend rather than break when rubbed. A delicious species, the Poplar Pholiota (*Agrocybe aegerita*) has a pale brown cap, which is almost white at maturity and a ringed stem of the same

colour, contrasting with gills which turn brown quickly. It often grows in large clumps, mainly on poplar. Many boletes are around this early. There is the Summer Bolete (*Boletus reticulatus*) which grows under deciduous trees and is distinguished from the Cep by its cap which is often grainy or velvety and is brown all over, even at the margin. The flesh, which soon becomes soft and wormy, is white under the cuticle of the cap and the stem is covered with a network almost from top to base. The Pinewood Bolete (*Boletus pinophilus*) is found under conifers. It is similar to the Cep but the cap and stem are redder. *Boletus erythropus* has a reddish-brown cap, which is matt in young specimens, then smooth. The pores are red and the stem is covered with tiny red dots. It is edible when well cooked, despite the way the flesh turns blue when cut. The delicious, fleshy, funnel-shaped Chanterelle (*Cantharellus cibarius*) is a beautiful orange-yellow colour all over. It has vestigial gills reduced to forked veins on the underside of the cap.

The fields and meadows are full of the Fairy Ring Champignon (*Marasmius oreades*), a small, delicate species which is reddish-brown all over and has a pleasant grassy smell which intensifies when it is dried out. The Champignon is a favourite filling for omelettes; the first Field Mushrooms (*Agaricus campestris*) will now be appearing on rich grassland.

Summer

JULY–AUGUST

During this period, fungi only appear after a storm. The species are much more varied, although Boletes, Russulas, Milk-caps and Amanitas tend to predominate. A few lignicolous* fungi, such as species of Marasmius and Pluteus, benefit from the water-retaining properties of wood in order to bear fruit. This is also the ideal time to study the fungus population which grows on hilltops and in the mountains.

In the Woods

The first Death Caps (*Amanita phalloides*) are starting to appear. The cap of this deadly fungus may be green in colour (olive green, yellowish-green or even greenish-brown) but there is also a white variety, which is usually radially striated with fine darker fibrils. The gills are always

white and the whitish stem has a ring tinged with green. The bulbous base is enveloped in a membranous volva. The common fleshy mushroom known as the Roll-rim (*Paxillus involutus*), which has a yellowish-brown velvety cap and yellow gills which brown quickly if they are rubbed, must also be avoided. It is very easy to spot thanks to the inrolled cap.

Of the various fungus curiosities which are not edible, there is also the Broad-Gilled Collybia (*Megacollybia platyphylla*) whose mycelium develops into thick, white rhizomorphs, the attractive clumps of Spindle Shank (*Collybia fusipes*) with its red-brown cap and deeply furrowed tapering stem, and the Fawn Pluteus (*Pluteus cervinus*), with its brown cap, pink gills and stem striped with fine brown fibrils and smell of radishes. There are also the rare Saffron Amanita (*Amanita crocea*), recognisable by its orange cap with its strongly striated margin, long, ringless stem flecked with orange patches and tight, white volva, the Fœtid Marasmius (*Micromphale foetidum*), identifiable by its reddish cap streaked with black and strong smell of cabbage, and the Yellow Staghorn (*Calocera viscosa*) which looks like a tiny, orange leafless bush, with its slimy, elastic flesh. Meals are made more interesting with the Wood Mushroom (*Agaricus silvicola*), whose white cap and stem turn yellow spontaneously or when rubbed, with its dark reddish-brown gills and marked smell of aniseed; *Boletus aereus*, a variety of Cep or Penny Bun Mushroom, with an almost black cap; the Bay Bolete (*Xerocomus badius*) whose cap and stem are chestnut-coloured and whose yellow pores turn blue when touched; and certain edible Russulas, including the Green Cracking Russula (*Russula virescens*), the common name of which describes its cracked green cap, and *Russula integra,* which grows in mountainous forests and has a cap of various shades of brown and gills which are cream-coloured at first then darken to yellow.

In the Meadows

There are some striking species, such as the Conical Wax-Cap (*Hygrocybe conica*), with its pointed, bright yellow and red cap, which blackens with age or if damaged, the Parrot Wax-Cap (*Hygrocybe psittacina*) whose slimy green cap is distinctive but when dry reveals a yellow

fungus underneath, and the Dung Roundhead (*Stropharia semiglobata*) with its hemispherical, slimy yellowish cap and ringed white stem which grows on dungheaps and manure as do the various species of Paneolus and Coprinus.

The Parasol Mushroom (*Macrolepiota procera*) can be seen from afar due to its large size. The cap can measure 30 cm (12 in) in diameter and the stem 30 cm (12 in), the latter decorated with brown flecks and a sliding ring. Only the cap is sufficiently tender to be worth eating. The Shaggy Ink Cap or Lawyer's Wig (*Coprinus comatus*) is easy to identify and also favours open ground. The cylindrical cap barely opens into an elongated bell and is covered in scales, but its gills are deliquescent which means they have an unfortunate tendency to decompose rapidly into a liquid which is blackened by the spores. Only young specimens are edible.

Autumn

SEPTEMBER–DECEMBER

Autumn is the favourite season for fungi and it is now that most species appear, in addition to those already mentioned whose growing season may extend into autumn. It is impossible to make a complete list, but some fungi deserve a special mention on account of their frequency, striking appearance, culinary importance or toxicity.

Under Broad-leaved Trees
BEECH

The most frequent species include Milk-caps, such as the Slimy Milk-cap (*Lactarius blennius*), whose cap is grey olive-brown in colour and often decorated with concentric splashes of darker colours. The stem is pale brown, contrasting with the white gills and the white milk, which turns olive-grey when dry, and the Pale Milk-cap (*Lactarius pallidus*), so called because of its overall pinkish-cream colour. There are numerous Russulas, the commonest of which are the Beech Russula (*Russula fageticola*) which has a striking bright red cap, white gills and stem, and very acrid flesh, and the Geranium-scented Russula (*Russula fellea*) which has an ochraceous-red cap and cream-coloured gills. The smell is also said to resemble apple sauce.

A few all-white fungi, which are easy to spot, are also encountered, including the Ivory Wax-cap (*Hygrophorus eburneus*), which is viscous and white all over, and which is said to smell of sticky tape(!) and, on the wood itself, the soft groups of the beautiful Porcelain Fungus (*Oudemansiella mucida*) with its ringed stem. The Magpie Cap (*Coprinus picaceus*) has a striking cap which is black covered with large white scales. The Cortinarius family is also represented with *Cortinarius elatior*, a large, viscous species whose brown cap is deeply wrinkled, and which has wide gills also wrinkled and a spindle-shaped stem; the Cinnabar Cortinarius (*Cortinarius cinnabarinus*) is visible from a long way away, as its fruiting body is entirely reddish-brown; the flesh smells of radishes. *Cortinarius calochrous* has a yellow cap which contrasts with violet gills and the bulbous stem has a flattened or marginated edge around the base. The Splendid Cortinarius (*Cortinarius splendens*), a highly suspect species which should not be eaten, has a bright yellow viscous cap, spotted with red and a cap of the same colour. The stem has a marginated base and the flesh is also yellow. The most unusual species is certainly the Pine-cone Bolete (*Strobilomyces strobilaceus*), which gets its name from its cap and stem covered in large blackish-brown scales.

Among the edible fungi, there is the Poets' Wax-cap (*Hygrophorus poetarum*) with its pinkish-ochre cap, pink gills and flesh and smell reminiscent of cinnamon. *Marasmius alliaceus* has a strong smell of garlic and can be used in the same way; its grey cap is supported on a long, thin brownish-black stem.

BIRCH

The large brown brackets with white undersides of the Birch Polypore (*Piptoporus betulinus*) appear on the tree trunks. On the ground, in addition to the poisonous Fly Agaric (*Amanita muscaria*), often found under birch, there are a few other inedible but interesting species such as the Woolly Milk-cap (*Lactarius torminosus*), remarkable for its pinkish-red cap with shaggy fibres at the margin; the Leaden Milk-cap (*Lactarius necator*), a large species, identifiable by its general olive-brown colour which is often very dark, and its white milk which turns violet in the presence of ammonia; *Lactarius glyciosmus,* which is much smaller and has a greyish-lilacine* cap, and has a strong odour of fig leaves;

Tricholoma fulvum, which is fawn-brown with bright yellow gills and yellow flesh that smells of flour; the Red-banded Cortinarius (*Cortinarius armillatus*), with a reddish cap and a beige stem ringed with bright red bands; there are a few boletes, including the Orange Birch Bolete (*Leccinum versipelle*), unmistakable with its bright-orange cap, grey pores, blackening white flesh and stem covered with tiny dark scales.

ALDER

The most typical species is the Livid Bolete (*Gyrodon lividus*), which is easy to recognise from its very short, decurrent* tubes; the Alder Pholiota (*Pholiota alnicola*), which grows in tufts and has a bright yellow cap which soon reddens, yellow, then rust-red gills, and a yellow stem which turns red at the base and has an annular area and a fruity smell like a boiled sweet; the Obscure Milk-cap (*Lactarius obscuratus*) whose orange-brown, umbonate cap is dark olive in the centre and whose sweet milk is opalescent; *Paxillus filamentosus*, recognisable by its decurrent brown gills which stain when touched, its yellow-brown cap dotted with loosely attached brown scales, and the cap margin striated with darker rings. These species are inedible.

OAK

Of the fungi which are common but inedible, there are the Lacquered Bracket (*Ganoderma lucidum*), which looks as if it has been entirely painted with lacquer, and which has a dark reddish-brown cap, attached at the side by a stem of the same colour and whitish pores; the Quiet Milk-cap (*Lactarius quietus*), with its zoned, reddish-brown cap whose stem is darker at the base, identifiable by its cream-coloured milk and strong smell said to be like that of wood-lice; the Yellow Milk-cap (*Lactarius chrysorrheus*), which is sometimes confused with the Saffron Milk-cap due to the concentric rings on its cap. However, it can be easily distinguished due to the white milk which turns golden-yellow in a few seconds. Two species, the Annatto-coloured Cortinarius (*Cortinarius orellanus*), with its velvety reddish-brown cap, and bright orange-fawn scales which turn rust-coloured, and the Livid Entoloma (*Entoloma sinuatum*), which is whitish-grey all over, with gills that are yellow at first, then pinkish-brown, and

whose flesh smells and tastes like flour, are poisonous and must be avoided.
Hygrophorus russula is covered with purple blotches on a pale background and is one of the most beautiful of the fungi that grow beneath oaks. It is edible.

POPLAR

In addition to the Poplar Pholiota which has already been mentioned, there is also the rather tough-fleshed bolete *Leccinum duriusculum*, which has a brown cap, whitish pores and a white stem typically covered with brown, flaky scales. The base of the stem is often stained with blue-green and the flesh is firm. There is also the Poplar Tricholoma (*Tricholoma populinum*), a fleshy species with pinkish-grey cap, a white stem turning to brown, whitish gills staining red and flesh with the smell and taste of flour.

SWEET CHESTNUT

In the autumn, *Rustroemia echinophila*, a sort of brown Elf-cup, may be found growing inside the husks. It is so small that several specimens may colonise a single fruit. It is of no culinary value.

Miscellaneous Broad-leaved Trees

There are far more fungi which are not tied exclusively to a particular species of broad-leaved tree.
The poisonous species include the Devil's Bolete (*Boletus satanas*). It has a large white cap covered in red pores, supported on a bulbous stem which is covered with a network of red lines against a yellow background. The flesh turns slightly blue when rubbed and it has a rubbery smell. It only grows on limestone. The Olive-tree Pleurotus (*Omphalotus olearius*) is also poisonous. It usually grows in clumps and is recognisable by its orange, funnel-shaped fruiting body and its decurrent gills of the same colour. Do not confuse it with the Chanterelle.
There are also a number of interesting but inedible fungi such as the Rooting Hebeloma (*Hebeloma radicosum*), whose cap is coffee-coloured and ringed stem radicant*; it smells strongly of bitter almonds. The Acrid Lactarius (*Lactarius acris*) is an uninteresting grey-brown colour all over but its white milk turns bright pink in the space of a few minutes; the Giant Fairy Club (*Clavariadelphus pistillaris*) is yellowish-brown.
On the other hand, the Amanita of the

Caesars (*Amanita caesarea*) can be eaten. It has an orange-coloured cap, yellow gills and stem and a ring. The stem is covered with a thick white volva*. It grows in forests in the south of France and tastes delicious. The Bleeding Agaric (*Agaricus haemorrhoidarius*) has a scaly brown cap and a ringed white stem; the flesh reddens strongly when touched. It is likewise suitable for eating as is also its close relative, the Field Mushroom. The Horn of Plenty (*Craterellus cornucopioides*), a funnel-shaped, grey-black fungus, goes well with meat gravy; the Cauliflower Clavaria (*Ramaria botrytis*) is also edible and recognisable by its thick white head, divided into flattish white branches which turn pink at the tops. The Beefsteak Fungus (*Fistulina hepatica*) is eaten cooked and sliced and is easily distinguishable by its dark red, warty cap, on a lateral stem, its pores which are not joined together and flesh which turns red when touched.

Under Conifers
LARCH

This is the tree favoured by the Larch Bolete (*Suillus grevillei*), the golden-yellow to orange-brown cap of which is slimy, and whose stem has a whitish annular area. The Hollow-stemmed Bolete (*Boletinus cavipes*) has a brown or bright yellow velvety cap, depending on the variety. The decurrent pores run down a hollow, ringed stem. The rare *Suillus tridentinus* has a slimy orange-to-rust-red cap and pores of the same colour which are decurrent on a ringed stem. The Viscous Bolete (*Suillus viscidus*) differs only in its generally more greyish-brown colour. *Lactarius porninsis* has an orange cap decorated with concentric rings or patches of colour. The stem is orange and has a very fruity smell; *Hygrophorus speciosus*, a magnificent hygrophorus, has a viscous yellow cap with a bright red-orange centre and a stem covered in patches of the slimy yellowish veil; *Gomphidius maculatus* has a brownish viscous cap which darkens in patches and grey decurrent gills which redden then blacken when touched. These species have no culinary value.

CEDARS

The most spectacular of these species is the Herculean Cortinarius (*Cortinarius herculeus*), which is brown all over but easily recognisable by its large size, its stem ringed with scaly bracelets and above all

its strong, penetrating earthy smell. It frequently grows alongside the Cedar Cortinarius (*Cortinarius cedretorum*) whose coppery cap has a yellow-green margin, a marginated bulb and violet flesh, and *Tricholoma tridentinum*, of which a variety grows under cedars, which has a slimy brown cap, cream-coloured gills, a whitish stem and smells strongly of flour. It often grows in tight clumps. These fungi are not worth picking.

SPRUCE

Most of the species which grow under spruce are inedible. They include the Spectacular Lactarius (*Lactarius repraesentaneus*), whose bright yellow cap has a hairy margin, and which has surprisingly white milk turning dark purple in a few minutes; *Lactarius scrobiculatus* has an orange-red cap with short hairs at the margin and a heavily pitted stem; the milk turns yellow when exposed to air. The Amethyst Russula (*Russula amethystina*), whose name derives from its maroon to violet cap, has butter-coloured gills and mild-flavoured flesh; *Cortinarius malicorius* has a reddish-brown matt cap which forms a contrast with the dark green flesh. *Russula mustelina* has an ochre-brown cap and cream-coloured gills and stem. It is edible and has firm, mild-tasting flesh; *Lactarius lignyotus* has an almost black velvety cap and stem, contrasting with its decurrent white gills which end in grooves on the stem. *Lactarius deterrimus* is edible despite its name and is a variety of the Saffron Milk-cap. However, it turns a more marked shade of green, the stem is ringed with white where the gills are attached to it, and the orange milk turns red in minutes.

PINES

Many fungi grow under pines. There are some interesting, inedible species such as the Pink Gomphidius (*Gomphidius roseus*) with its pink or dark red, viscous cap, white stem and white decurrent gills which soon turn grey when covered with ripe spores; *Lactarius hepaticus* which has shades of brown mixed with green and white milk turning yellow; the Sanguine Russula (*Russula sanguinaria*) whose cap and stem are blood-red, with cream-coloured gills and acrid flesh; *Russula xerampelina*, similar to the previous species but notable for its unpleasant fishy smell; *Russula torulosa*, which has a dark violet cap and a violet stem, contrasting with

cream-coloured gills which smell strongly of apples; *Russula drimeia*, whose cap and stem colour resemble those of the previous species but whose gills are lemon-yellow, turning red in ammonia vapour. There is also *Suillus bovinus*, a soft-fleshed bolete with a slimy cap and generally brownish colour. It has large composite pores, that is to say they subdivide into smaller pores. The best species for eating are the Woolly Milk-cap (*Lactarius deliciosus*), with its ringed cap, which is orange like the rest of the fungus, and its carrot-coloured milk, which does not change colour on exposure to the air, and *Lactarius vinosus*, which looks very similar and is also edible, but which is more maroon in colour, especially the scales, and whose milk is also darker. There is also Slippery Jack (*Suillus luteus*), which is easy to recognise from its slimy, chocolate-brown cap, yellow pores and a yellowish stem with darker granulations above a large ring which is white at first, turning violet.

Miscellaneous Conifers

Among those species which are not strictly tied to a particular conifer, there is the Red Milk-cap (*Lactarius rufus*), whose dark red cap is umbonate*, with a paler stem and white, very acrid milk; *Tricholoma aurantium* which has a slimy orange cap and a white stem splashed with viscous rings of the same colour as the cap, and a strong smell of cucumber; *Hygrophorus agathosmus*, with its viscous, grey cap and decurrent gills which are white like the stem; it smells of bitter almonds or rubber cement. The deceptively named Plums and Custard (*Tricholomopsis rutilans*) is inedible and grows on stumps. The cap is covered with purple patches against a yellow background. The gills and flesh are yellow and bitter-tasting.

There are also some delicious fungi, such as *Tricholoma portentosum*, whose slimy grey, yellow-tinged cap is decorated with radial fibrils. The white stem and gills are washed with lemon-yellow; the flesh smells of oysters. The Jelly Tongue (*Pseudohydnum gelatinosum*) grows on wood. The cap is brown and is covered in grey spines. The fungus can be eaten raw in salads. There is also the Cauliflower Fungus (*Sparassis crispa*) whose mass of tightly packed wrinkled lobes resembles those of a cauliflower.

Fungi

Conifers and Miscellaneous Broad-leaved Trees

There are fungi which have no particular preference for a species of tree and will grow in mixed woods.

These include the Death Cap and another species to be avoided at all costs, *Galerina marginata*, also known as *Galerina unicolor*, which grows on rotten wood. It is brown all over, turning paler when dry, and the stem has a small ring. The fungus tastes and smells floury. The Tiger Tricholoma (*Tricholoma pardinum*) has a fleshy grey cap which can attain 15 cm (6 in) in diameter and is covered with darker scales; it, too, smells floury. All the tiny Lepiotas are poisonous or suspect, such as the Stinking Parasol (*Lepiota cristata*), whose pale cap has a central red disk and reddish concentric scales, with white gills and stem. The stem has a funnel-shaped ring and the fungus has a rubbery smell. The various white species of Clitocybe and Inocybe also grow in mixed woods.

The Stinking Russula (*Russula fœtens*) has a viscous, reddish-yellow cap which is deeply grooved at the margin; the stem and flesh are paler in colour and it has a strongly fœtid odour. *Boletus calopus* has a whitish cap, bright yellow pores and a red stem covered with a white mesh; the flesh turns bright blue when cut but is bitter. This is one of those species which is easy for the amateur to identify but unfortunately it is inedible.

However, *Tricholoma atrosquamosum* is very good to eat, with a cap covered in small blackish scales, whitish gills sometimes edged with black, a whitish stem which may be scaly and flesh with a peppery smell. *Tricholoma equestre* has a dirty yellow cap tinged with red in the centre, sulphur-yellow gills, a paler stem and a floury smell. The Aniseed Toadstool (*Clitocybe odora*) has a greenish cap and stem; the paler gills are decurrent and smell strongly of aniseed; the Wood Hedgehog (*Hydnum repandum*) has an orange cap covering a hymenium consisting of small paler spines. The Amethyst Deceiver (*Laccaria amethystina*) is entirely violet, with a matt cap and thick, widely spaced gills. The Wood Blewit (*Lepista nuda*) has a cap which is violet then brown, a violet stem and violet gills which can be peeled away in one go like the choke of an artichoke.

Open Ground

Open grassland (meadows, lawns, roadside verges, the grassy edges of cultivated fields, etc.) are often places where interesting fungi can be found.

This is the favourite habitat for another poisonous small Lepiota species, *Lepiota brunneoincarnata*, the cap of which tears into little reddish-brown scales. The gills are whitish and the stem is white at the top and has a fat bolster-shaped ring below which there is an area covered with flecks the same colour as the cap. The Yellow-Staining Mushroom (*Agaricus xanthoderma*) should not be eaten. It is very closely related to the Cultivated Mushroom and the Field Mushroom but can easily be recognised because the flesh turns bright yellow at the base of the stem and has a chemical smell a little like poster paint.

The most frequently encountered species include *Stropharia coronilla*, which has a yellow cap, violet-brown gills and a white stem with a striped ring.

Two edible Wax-caps grow on grassland. One is the Crimson Wax-cap (*Hygrocybe punicea*), with its fleshy red cap, yellowish gills and orange stem covered in red fibrils, and the other is the Meadow Wax-cap (*Hygrocybe pratensis*), a drab orange colour. The Horse Mushroom (*Agaricus arvensis*) is easily recognised by its ring which looks like a gear-wheel and its smell of aniseed; there is also the Giant Puffball (*Langermannia gigantea*) which can grow to a size at which it weighs several kilograms and is edible when young and the spores are white.

UNUSUAL HABITATS

Some fungi grow in unusual places.

For instance, *Leucocoprinus flossulfuris* is a brilliant, sulphur-coloured Lepiota which grows in flower-pots or under glass. Dry Rot (*Serpula lacrymans*) is the notoriously destructive fungus which favours damp houses and destroys the wood, causing a reddish rot. It looks like a folded, spongy mass, with a rust-coloured mass of pores and a white margin.

The fungal flora of slag heaps and the galleries of mines are also interesting sites in which to study fungi, as are all types of burned ground. Where cultivated land or forest has been burned down, either deliberately as part of slash-and-burn agriculture or accidentally through a forest fire, the habitat favours the appearance of the Charcoal Pholiota (*Pholiota highlandensis*), a gilled fungus with a coppery-brown cap covered with a slimy, elastic pellicle* which is easily removable.

Heim's Inocybe (*Inocybe heimii*) grows in sand-dunes by the sea. It has a woolly, reddish-ochre cap and a fibrillous stem ringed with a thick woolly fold; *Hygrocybe conicoides* looks very much like the Conical Wax-cap (*Hygrocybe conica*) but is strictly arenicolous*; the Sand Elf-Cap (*Peziza ammophila*) consists of a brown cup on a stem which is entirely buried in the sand.

Peat bogs containing sphagnum moss can also contain unusual species such as the Marsh Mitrula (*Mitrula paludosa*), an orange-yellow Fairy Club with a whitish stem and soft, slimy texture, or the Marsh Galerina (*Galerina paludosa*) with a brick-red cap, striated margin, reddish gills and a long stem of the same colour, ringed with white patches. The Sphagnum Omphalia (*Omphalina sphagnicola*) looks like a tiny Clitocybe which is grey all over and has very decurrent gills; the cap has blackish scales in the centre. Some fungi can be identified merely from their unusual habitat. An example of this is the Parasitical Bolete (*Xerocomus parasiticus*) which grows on Earth-balls (fungi that are similar to Puffballs but with a thick, warty skin and black interior); another is the Parasitical Nyctalis (*Nyctalis parasitica*), a tiny white-gilled fungus which grows on old Russulas. The Caterpillar Fungus (*Cordyceps militaris*) is a bright red Fairy Club which grows on the larvae of buried insects, usually flies. None of these species is edible.

Index

Glossary

Arenicolous: growing in sand.

Compost: organic substances which become humus as they break down.

Cortinaceous: covered in a cortina, a very fine veil, extending between the edge of the cap and the stem.

Cuticle: thin skin covering the cap.

Decurrent: used to describe gills, tubes or spines which run down the stem from the underside of the cap.

Fimicolous: growing on dung or on soil rich in manure.

Hygrophanous: changing colour as it dries.

Hymenium: the spore-bearing surface of the fruiting body.

Lignicolous: growing on wood.

Lilacine: shading to lilac.

Margin: the edge of the cap.

Pellicle: thin coating or skin on the cap.

Phanera: protective elements produced by the skin such as hairs, nails, feathers, etc.

Radicant: used to describe a stem which extends deep into the growing medium somewhat like a root.

Septate: partitioned internally.

Squamose: scaly.

Umbonate: having a small boss or umbo in the centre of the cap.

Volva: membrane which entirely covers some fungi at their young stage but which tears as they grow. It sometimes persists in the adult form as a sac at the base of the stem or as patches on the cap.

Bibliography

Books

Andary, Privat & Rascol, *Les Intoxications par les champignons*, Faculté de Pharmacie de Montpellier, 1991.

Bon M., *Champignons d'Europe occidentale*, Arthaud, 1988.

Courtecuisse R & Duhem B., *Les champignons de France*, Eclectis, 1994.

Fourré G., *Pièges et curiosités des champignons*, 1990.

Harding, P. and Lyon, T., *Edible Mushrooms* (HarperCollins, 1996)

Harding, P., *Mushrooms and Toadstools Photoguide* (HarperCollins, 1996)

Læssøe, T. and Conte, A. del, *The Mushroom Book* (Dorling Kindersley, 1996)

Læssøe, T., *Mushrooms* (Dorling Kindersley, 1998)

Marchand A., *Champignons du Nord et du Midi*, vols. 1–9, Société Mycologique des Pyrénées Méditerranéennes, 1971–1986.

Moser M. & Jülich W., *Farbatlas der Basidiomyceten*, vols. 1–15, Gustav Fischer Verlag, 1985–1997.

Pegler, D., *Field Guide to Mushrooms and Toadstools* (1998)

Phillips R., *Les Champignons*, Solar, 1981.

Phillips R., *Mushrooms and Other Fungi of Great Britain and Europe* (Pan, 1981)

Phillips R., *Wild Food* (Pan, 1983)

Romagnesi H., *Petit atlas des champignons*, vols. 1–2, Bordas, 1970–1971.

Specialist periodicals

Bulletin Trimestriel de la Fédération Mycologique Dauphiné-Savoie.

Bulletin Trimestriel de la Société Mycologique de France, Paris.

Documents Mycologiques, Association d'Écologie et de Mycologie, Lille.

Bulletin Semestriel de la Fédération des Associations Mycologiques Méditerranéennes, Montpellier.

Zeitschrift für Mykologie, Germany.

Mycological Research, United Kingdom.

Mycologist, The International Journal of General Mycology, United Kingdom.

McIlvainea, Journal of American Amateur Mycology, USA.

Acknowledgements

The author thanks Serge Kizlik, an excellent mycologist, who showed him the multiple facets of mycology and helped him with the creation of this book. He also thanks all those who were kind enough to read the manuscript.